KIDCRAFT
TREASURY

KIDCRAFT TREASURY

The *Woman's Day®* Book of Fun Projects for Kids

MEREDITH® PRESS

NEW YORK

For Hachette Magazines, Inc.
Editor-in-Chief, Woman's Day: Ellen R. Levine
Editorial Project Director: Geraldine Rhoads
Editor: Lina Morielli
Instructions: Ellen W. Liberles

For Meredith® Press
Director: Elizabeth F. Rice
Assistant: Ruth Weadock
Editorial Project Manager: Connie Schrader
Editorial Assistant: Carolyn Mitchell
Project Editor: Bob Oskam
Production Manager: Bill Rose

Distributed by Meredith Corporation
Des Moines, Iowa

ISBN: 0-696-02346-6

Library of Congress Catalog Card Number: 90-063668

Printed in the United States of America

10 9 8 7 6 5 4 3 2 1

Design by Stanley S. Drate, Folio Graphics Co. Inc.

Packaged by Rapid Transcript, a division of March Tenth, Inc.

CONTENTS

JUST FOR FUN

FUN FOR SPECIAL OCCASIONS

GENERAL DIRECTIONS

Acknowledgments

Thousands upon thousands of children have learned the fun and satisfaction of creating things from the crafts pages in *Woman's Day.* This collection is a gathering of favorites: traditional projects updated, recent projects, plus brand-new items developed for this book.

Three specialists are key contributors to the book:

The editor, Lina Morielli, was for ten years associate needlework and crafts editor of *Woman's Day,* and designed twenty-five of the projects in these pages. Since leaving the magazine, moving from New York to spend more time with her son, Zachary, now eight years old, she has freelanced as a crafts designer, editor, and consultant for magazines, yarn companies, advertising and public relations companies, and marketing firms. She considers herself a craft generalist, "a Jill of all trades," if you will. She is a graduate of Parsons School of Design, with a specialty in graphic communications.

Instruction specialist Ellen Liberles also spent a major portion of her career at *Woman's Day*—fifteen years in all, principally as an instruction writer. She also served as Assistant Fashion Director at a yarn company, and worked on the *Vogue* knitting book. She has traveled throughout Europe, South America, Africa, the Orient, Mexico, Australia, and New Zealand, pursuing an interest in folk-art crafts and designs. A mother of two—both sons are now in college—Ellen "served time" as a Cub Scout den mother ("the hardest job I've ever had!") and introduced her own children to crafts. She is a Dickinson College graduate and has also studied clothing construction, home crafts, decorating and child development at Pennsylvania State College.

Artist and art educator Dolores Olson, who has taught in public and private schools for thirty years, is represented by eleven projects in this book. Her appointments have included the crafts directorship of a children's day center serving three hundred campers ranging in age from five to sixteen. She is the co-author of *Big Ideas for Little People,* a 1985 book based on ABC-TV's Saturday children's special "The Littles." When ABC-TV sought a crafts designer for that show, the Board of Education recommended her; she continues with the network, as a consultant for other children's projects. She has two daughters, both engaged in careers outside the crafts area, "leaving my specialty to me."

PHOTOGRAPHERS

Didier Dorot: Shell and Feather Animals, Water Scope, Pretend Beach Sailboat

Julie Gang: Wooden-Spoon Puppets, Newspaper Hat, Puff-Paint Sweatshirt, Button Necklace and Barrette, Bean Necklace, Tie-dyed T-shirts, Shadow Drawing, Pea and Toothpick Creation, Tick-tack-toe Game, Fruit and Vegetable Prints, Leaf Prints, Soap Dish, Valentine Crown, Loving Cup

Andre Guillardin: Easy Gingerbread Houses

Frances McLaughlin: Kitten Mask, Hound Mask

The rest of the photographs are the work of *Woman's Day* staff photographer Ben Calvo.

DESIGNERS

Amy Albert Bloom: Wind Sock

Yvonne Beecher: Puff-Paint Sweatshirt, Puff-Paint Sneakers

Martha Jocelyn: Jumping Jack, Wooden-Spoon Puppets, Button Necklace and Barrette, Bean Necklace

Lina Morielli: Paper Bag Clown, Newspaper Hat, Sand Sunburst, Leaf Prints, Leaf Rubbing, Folded-Hands Valentine, Heart Stickers

Pot, Valentine Crown, Hanging Basket, Loving Cup, Eraser-Print Stationery, Found-Object Picture Rubbing, Soap Dish, Candy Bauble Square, Candy Bauble Tree, Popcorn and Gumdrop Wreath, Glitter Star, Paper Snowflakes, Sticker Lotto, Dinosaur Pins, Sponge-Print Wrapping Paper, Paperweights, Pop-up Santa Card, Pop-up Christmas Tree Card, Macaroni Star

Dolores Olson: Stretchable Crocodile and Clown, Tiny Spool Dolls, Dudley Spool Dragon, Shell and Feather Animals, Rock Village, Shell Pins and Magnets, Shell Catchall, Shell and Pompon Snake, Sand Castle Pencil Holder, Birds in Branches, String Picture

Joanne Sanders: Easy Gingerbread Houses

Ginger Hansen Schaffer: Tie-dyed T-shirts, Fruit and Vegetable Prints

Mavis Smith: Kitten Mask, Hound Mask

Ternion Designs: Pretend Beach Sailboat by Brent Pallas

Dear Crafter Parent:

Mastering new skills promotes a special excitement and feelings of self-confidence. KIDCRAFT TREASURY, developed by *Woman's Day* magazine, presents a wide range of exciting projects to expand your child's natural creativity and imagination while providing hours of wholesome fun.

Children of every age enjoy making their own dolls, toys, and games. It is with that in mind that we offer this treasure trove of fun—more than sixty creative projects. The level of skill required to complete each project is indicated clearly. Twelve-year-olds will find many projects anticipating their level of skill, as will younger children. A young child not yet able to read and follow written instructions will find photographs clear enough to serve as a reliable guide (with a responsible adult always at hand to ensure safety).

We at Meredith Press are pleased to bring you KIDCRAFT TREASURY. Our aim is always to provide our readers a variety of projects, with clear, practical directions on how to get the results pictured. We enjoyed working out the simple steps in making a game, toy, or present that looks every bit as good as in our photographs. The full-size patterns, helpful diagrams, and clear, full-color photographs are just what is needed to tempt any child into happy hours of crafting.

We hope you and your family enjoy our treasury of imaginative activities.

Sincerely,
CONNIE SCHRADER, *Editorial Project Manager*

INTRODUCTION

"I made it myself!"

It is a pleasure to be able to say this at almost any age, but unalloyed joy for a child who sees something materialize out of his or her own efforts. A youngster's eyes light up all the more if people praise what he or she has done, but it is not all that important that other people like it. What counts is the child's satisfaction in mastering a technique, in seeing what he or she can do.

Children should be pleased with what they are doing. That means beginning with something they are interested in doing and can manage without too much difficulty.

So your very first move in engaging your child's interest is to have the child select a project he or she can complete successfully.

WHAT WILL BE FUN FOR YOUR CHILD?

All children are creative, but no two are equally skilled. You can't classify one project as right for five-year-olds and another as suitable for eight-year-olds, and the worst thing is to push a young child into doing what older children do before he or she is ready for it.

It's useless to offer a child any experience with arts and crafts materials until he or she can handle them constructively—that is, not until after you see the child holding objects and at least trying to handle them as you direct. If your child pours paint on the table, throws materials around, or eats them rather than tries to use them correctly, wait a bit. Your child will be ready soon enough. I have taught nursery school children as young as three and a half years old to make simple crafts. But expect some awkwardness at first. You and I may be used to arts and crafts materials, but children, though thrilled with this new adventure in making things themselves, are at first dazzled and a bit confused by the materials.

Because no two children are alike, let your child be your guide as to when he or she is ready to begin specific crafts. If your child really is a beginner or feels unsure of how to proceed, it sometimes helps to make a separate project of your own along with the child. This gives the child the chance to learn by watching you and still have the experience of doing his or her own craft.

The three ratings accompanying our projects—Experienced, Intermediate, and Beginner—are broad guidelines. They alert you when items require a little more strength or greater motor skills, demand the use of adult tools, or involve a longer attention span. But look at the materials lists and instructions yourself to decide if, for example, a project for the "experienced" is really too demanding for your little girl or boy. Some of the features for "beginners"—especially our Easter and Christmas items—may be just right for occasions when children of different ages share an afternoon or evening of crafts-making.

In my experience, children capable of executing advanced projects also have fun with an easy one, because they can embellish an item to suit their creative bent. They add beads or feathers or develop a more intricate design.

I'm often asked what to do if a child falls in love with something that a parent thinks is beyond his or her abilities. That always reminds me of the time I had some five-year-olds making biplanes out of Popsicle sticks. These were intricate projects requiring concentration for many hours. But we went ahead and made the biplanes anyway. We completed them in a week by working on them in one-hour sessions.

If children are enthusiastic enough about a big challenge, they are usually motivated to see it through. It's a good idea, though, to be sure that they go at it in an orderly way. Break the project into many steps. A step at a time is not so overwhelming as to discourage them.

In fact, one of the lessons children take from making crafts is the value of logical thinking, that Step 1 comes before Step 2. The eager child gains a sense of confidence and competence when he or she successfully completes each step, working at his or her own speed, with enough support so there is no fear of failing or going wrong.

THE IMPORTANCE OF ENCOURAGEMENT

Play is a serious matter for children; it fulfills their need to express themselves. You help most when you try to understand what your child is trying to do and regard what he or she does as valuable. Try to look at what your child shows you with an understanding eye. Rather than criticize an awkwardly constructed item, praise the effort. A disparaging remark, even simple indifference, can discourage a child from developing the creative initiative that is part of healthy self-expression.

You encourage a child most when you watch as he or she works. Attentiveness on your part is as telling as your praises for the final product.

That doesn't mean you must hover over a young crafter all the time. It is, of course, not possible or even necessary for busy parents to be with children every minute they are constructing. But being available makes a child more confident; it helps if your child just knows you're *there*.

You don't have to do crafts work for the child (unless you take over some steps for safety's sake), and in fact you *mustn't* take over the work of making the item. That only questions the child's ability and robs him or her of the adventure of making something new.

YOUR ROLE AS TEACHER

In introducing your child to crafts work, you become a teacher. You teach techniques that facilitate creative self-expression. Children are proud when they master these, especially when they can go off on their own and create something new to surprise you.

You teach them how to use tools, eventually introducing them to the tools adults use, and show them how to keep tools in condition so they're fun to work with again and again. (Your young students may pick up a few rudimentary lessons in housekeeping, too, along the way!)

The art of teaching is giving someone the chance and the encouragement to learn something.

When children work with various materials of different textures, patterns, and colors, they are developing a sensitivity to the quality of materials.

When your boy or girl arranges and rearranges such things as pebbles and nuts into a design, he or she is developing personal creative power. The child is discovering how to express ideas and feelings with materials readily at hand.

Growth manifests itself in a variety of ways. When encouraged to work in their own way, children will grow in independence. Not only will they ask for less help, but they will be able to get started more easily and be less distracted. As they work with greater sureness and absorption, their ideas will flow more freely and they will become less and less concerned with standards other than their own.

One way to define crafts creativity is to say that it is simply the putting together of two or more materials to create something uniquely new.

When you give a child the opportunity to do that, you encourage the development of an adventurous outlook that will profit him or her in adult life.

You will use this book to best advantage if you encourage the boy or girl who undertakes projects in it to make them with whatever embellishments he or she fancies. A child's creation can look like ours or, with distinctive personal touches, look even better. Encourage a child who has completed a project to go on to make an original creation with leftover supplies. Challenge the child's imagination.

Your children may not grow up to be crafts professionals, but they may take career-enhancing abilities into adult life. I know a surgeon who made sure his son learned to knit, in order to develop the manual strength and dexterity that so well serve a surgeon. In any case, as a result of these relaxed and pleasurable sessions in childhood, your children will know what an agreeable pastime crafts can be.

There is great satisfaction and creative outlet for the adult who can relax with fine woodworking or decorative needlecraft, view the finished work and, with the same pleasure felt by a child, proudly say, "I made it myself."

—DOLORES OLSON

Instructions for prints such as are used at right are given in our chapter "Stamping and Rubbing."

JUST
FOR FUN

PAPER BAG CLOWN

BEGINNER

Stuff a paper bag with newspaper, glue it to a cardboard platform. Decorate and you've got a funny clown for the playroom.

You will need:

Paper lunch bag
Construction paper in various colors
Newspaper
4-inch by 6-inch piece of cardboard
Tracing paper
White glue or glue stick
Blunt scissors
Pencil
Compass or round plates

1 Stuff the paper bag with pieces of crumpled newspaper. Twist the top of the bag tightly closed.

2 Trace the patterns (see "How to Trace and Use Your Patterns," page 163), and then cut the pieces from construction paper. To get eyes and eyebrows the same shape, cut in pairs, holding two pieces of paper together as you cut. Cut out circles for the nose and cheeks.

3 Glue the cheeks, the eyes, eyebrows, and then the mouth, which covers part of the cheeks.

4 Glue a small roll of paper behind the nose circle for a 3-D look. Glue to the head.

5 Cut several 3-inch by 6-inch strips of construction paper for hair. Following the diagram, cut closely spaced slits into one end of the paper strips. Curl by rolling the slit ends around a pencil.

6 Glue the uncut end of the hair strips to the head, then glue the ear tabs over the hair and fold the ears to stick out.

15

7 For the hat, trace around a dinner plate to draw a circle on construction paper; cut out the circle. Following the hat diagram, cut away a quarter-circle wedge. Overlap the edges and glue to form a cone.

8 Cut a 3-inch by 4-inch strip of construction paper for hat trim. Slit one end as you did for the hair.

9 Snip off the tip of the cone hat. Roll or fold the uncut end of the hat trim to fit through the hole; glue the end inside the hat. Glue the hat over the twisted top of the bag.

10 For the collar circles, use a compass or trace around large lids to draw three slightly different size circles on construction paper; cut out the circles.

11 Glue the collar circles together with the smallest one centered on top. Glue the circles to the bottom of the bag. Glue the cardboard piece centered underneath for a base.

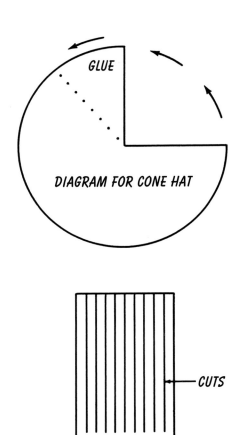

GLUE

DIAGRAM FOR CONE HAT

CUTS

DIAGRAM FOR HAIR

PAPER BAG CLOWN

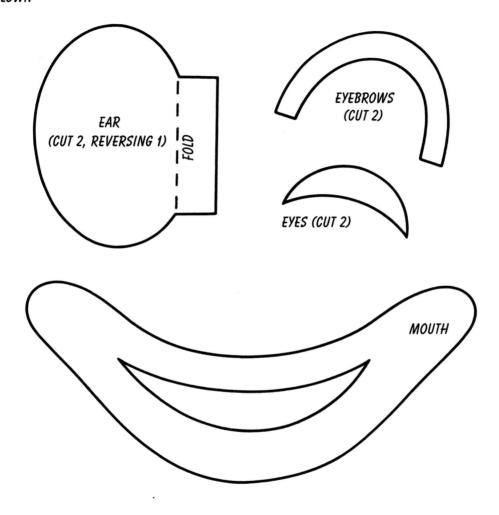

EAR
(CUT 2, REVERSING 1)

FOLD

EYEBROWS
(CUT 2)

EYES (CUT 2)

MOUTH

NEWSPAPER HAT

BEGINNER

A "pretend-Indian" topper, easy for a new crafter to fold, glue, paint . . . and then wear to a party, or out to play any day.

You will need:

Large-size newspaper
Poster paints in assorted colors
Paintbrushes, 1 inch to 2 inches wide
Feathers
4-inch foam ball
Crepe paper streamers
Glitter
White glue
Blunt scissors
Stapler
Yardstick
Serrated knife to cut foam ball

1 Use two full-size sheets of newspaper folded in pages as they come. Measure and cut 3 inches off one end to make 14-inch by 19-inch sheets.

2 Following the diagram, lay the paper with the fold at the top. Turn down the top corners to meet at the center, leaving several inches of paper below for the brim.

3 At the bottom of the hat, fold up half of the extra part of the top two sheets (as along the bottom dotted line on the diagram). Then fold up again (as along the second dotted line) to form a brim on one side. Turn the hat over and fold up a brim on that side. Staple the ends of the brim together. Glue the ends of two crepe paper streamers inside the brim at the center back of the hat.

4 Paint and decorate your hat as you wish. *Tips*: Paint different parts of the hat in different colors. Squeeze on glue in lines around some of the colored sections and sprinkle these lines with glitter. Let the glue dry (about an hour) before moving. Tuck the ends of the feathers under the brim and staple them in place. Have an adult cut a foam ball in half with a serrated knife. Apply glue to the cut sides of the ball, stick them on the brim and hold them in place until dry.

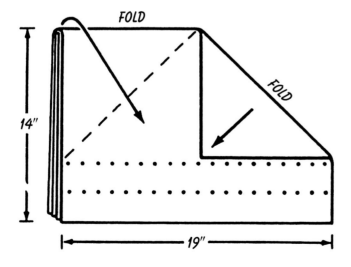

FOLD

FOLD

14"

19"

NEWSPAPER HAT

FULL-OF-BEANS BEAR

INTERMEDIATE

Introduce a child to sewing with this toy project. Glued features do the rest to give our chubby pet a smile.

You will need:

Two 7-inch squares of felt for the
    body
Scraps of felt in assorted colors for
    eyes, nose, ears, muzzle, paws,
    and tummy
1 yard of yarn
Large-eyed needle
Dried beans
White glue
Blunt scissors
Tracing paper

1 Trace the bear pattern (see "How to Trace and Use Your Patterns," page 163). Trace separate patterns for the face, ears, paws, and tummy.

2 Cut a bear body from each felt square, making two bodies. Cut the muzzle, ears, paws, nose, mouth, and tummy from the scraps of felt.

3 Glue the muzzle, two ears, two paws, and tummy in place on one felt body.

4 Place the bear bodies together back to back. Thread the yarn through the large-eyed needle. Starting at the neck and leaving a 6-inch yarn end, sew evenly and closely spaced running stitches about ¼ inch in from the edge all around the bear to within 2 inches of the place where you started.

5 Stuff the bear with the dried beans.

6 Sew the last 2 inches closed. Tie the yarn ends into a bow, cutting off any extra yarn.

FULL-OF-BEANS BEAR

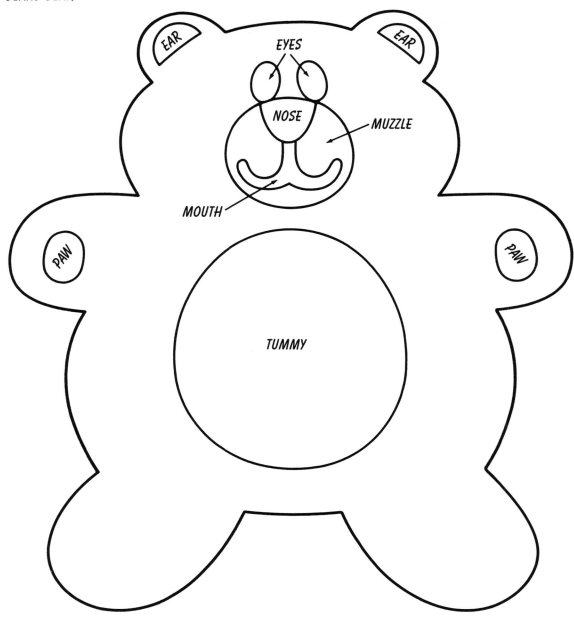

Wooden-Spoon Puppets

EXPERIENCED

The young dramatist can spend days in Make-Believe Land with these cheery characters. The spoons come from the kitchen, the scraps of felt, yarn, and ribbon from Mom's sewing box.

For each puppet, you will need:

Wooden spoon, 15 to 18 inches long
7-inch by 15-inch piece of cloth
Felt scraps in assorted colors
Yarn for the girl's hair
12-inch length of 1/4- to 3/8-inch-wide
   ribbon for hair bows
Tracing paper
Black felt-tipped marker
Sewing needle
Thread
Blunt scissors

1 With the marker, draw a face on the back of the spoon.

2 Make a narrow hem along one 15-inch edge of the cloth. With the wrong side out, sew the narrow ends of the cloth together with a 1/4-inch-wide seam. Turn right side out.

3 Sew a row of running stitches along the unhemmed edge of the cloth, and gather tightly around the "neck" of the spoon.

4 Trace the collar pattern (see "How to Trace and Use Your Patterns," page 163), and cut a collar from the felt. Glue the long straight edge around the neck, covering the edge and the gathers of cloth at the neckline.

5 Trace the hand pattern and cut two hands from the felt. Glue a hand to each side of the skirt as shown in the photograph.

6 For the clown, trace the hat and brim patterns and cut the pieces from the felt. Cut small felt circles for the hat, buttons, cheeks, and nose. Glue all the pieces in place.

7 For the girl, cut nine 12-inch strands of yarn. Tie the strands together at the center with a separate double strand of yarn. Trim the tie ends to 1 inch for the bangs. On each side of the center tie, divide the strands into three groups of three strands each and braid loosely (see "How to Braid," page 163). With a 6-inch length of the narrow ribbon, tie a bow at the end of each braid. Glue the center of the hair to the top of the spoon with the bangs at the front.

WOODEN SPOON PUPPETS

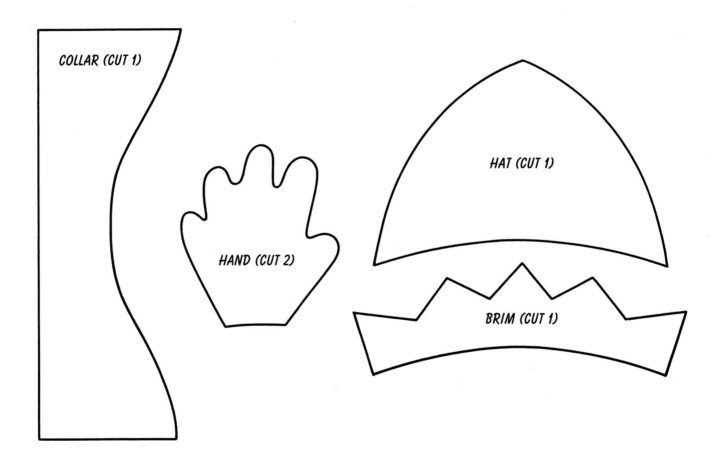

COLLAR (CUT 1)

HAND (CUT 2)

HAT (CUT 1)

BRIM (CUT 1)

STICKER LOTTO

It's a cinch to make lotto boards and cards with stickers. Then play away! (Lotto playing instructions included.)

You will need:

Several large sheets of poster board
Identical pairs of stickers with
    assorted shapes and designs
    (have two and only two of each
    different sticker design)
3-inch by 5-inch plain white file
    cards
White glue
Pencil
Blunt scissors
Ruler

1   Cut poster board into 12-inch by 17¾-inch rectangles to make a board for each player.

2   For each board, cut twenty file cards in half to make 2½-inch by 3-inch rectangles. Following the picture, arrange half of the white cards in five evenly spaced rows of four cards each, leaving about ¼ inch between them. Glue the cards in place.

3   Attach a different sticker to each rectangle on the boards, and attach the matching sticker to one of the remaining cards.

HOW TO PLAY LOTTO

You will need two or more players. Each player has a board. Lay the cards, sticker-side down, in the middle of the table. Each player in turn picks up a card. If it matches a sticker on his or her board, the child places the card over the matching sticker and then picks up a new card from the center pile. As long as a player can match each new card to an identical sticker on his or her board, the player continues to pick up cards. A player's turn is over when he or she draws a card that doesn't match his or her board. The next player is the person to the left of the last player. The next player picks a new card, or, if a previous player drew a card that matches, the next player can call for it and then continue to pick new cards as long as they match his or her board. Play continues until one player covers his or her board with matching cards.

Dudley Spool Dragon

Dudley is a friendly dragon who costs next to nothing to make. Spools, a clothespin, and googly eyes are all you need to assemble this little playmate.

You will need:

Empty thread spools, as many as
  you'd like
Brightly colored wooden beads
1 yard of nylon kite string or other
  strong string (for threading)
Three wooden spring-type
  clothespins
Two small red pompons
Two movable eyes (available at crafts
  supply stores)
Scrap of red felt
White glue
Blunt scissors

1 Thread one end of the string through a bead. Bring the end up and knot it to the string just above the bead (see diagram). Trim this short end close to the knot. Add a dab of glue to the cut end to keep the string from unraveling.

2 Starting from the tail, thread the spools onto the string, always with a bead between. If you have different-size spools, use the smallest ones first for the tail and the largest ones last. Thread, alternating spools and beads, until Dudley grows to the size you want.

3 Knot the string next to the last bead you have threaded, leaving the string just loose enough to allow the spools to wiggle.

4 Leaving a 2-inch end above the knot, trim off the extra string.

5 Have an adult help to remove the metal spring from the clothespins. Glue together the edges of two wooden halves, side by side, for the lower jaw. Glue two more halves together for the snout. Glue the flat side of another half to the top of the snout for a ridge.

6 Glue an eye on each pompon and then glue a pompon on each side of the snout, as shown.

7 With the 2-inch end of string sandwiched between, glue the grooved ends of the jaw and snout together as shown.

8 Cut a narrow strip of red felt and glue to the lower jaw for the tongue.

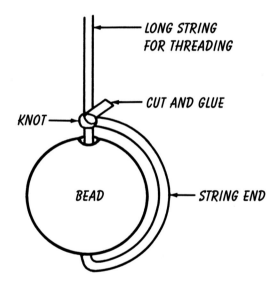

LONG STRING FOR THREADING

CUT AND GLUE

KNOT

BEAD

STRING END

JUMPING JACK

EXPERIENCED

This lively toy made of poster board has arms and legs that jump up and down.

You will need:

Poster board in various colors
24-inch length of string
Four paper fasteners measuring
   ½ inch to 1 inch
11-inch length of ¼-inch-diameter
   dowel
Black felt-tipped marker
White glue
Tracing paper
Blunt scissors
Pencil
Paper punch
Large-eyed needle

1 Trace pattern shapes onto poster board (see "How to Trace and Use Your Patterns," page 163). Cut out carefully.

2 Punch holes for the fasteners at the small circles and poke out the holes with the needle at the dots on the arms and legs. This is where the string will go.

3 Draw the eyes and a mouth on the face with the felt-tipped marker.

4 Following the dotted lines on the patterns, overlap the edges and glue the hat to the face. Next glue the face to the collar. Then glue the collar to the body.

5 Glue the dowel to the center back of the body and head. Let the glue dry.

6 Join the legs and the arms to the body with paper fasteners.

7 Thread the string into the needle and knot the end. Working at the back of the toy, push the needle down through the small hole on one arm and up through the small hole on the other arm. Knot the string, leaving 3 inches between the arms (see diagram). Cut off the extra string.

8 Knot the end of the string again, and push the needle down through the hole on one leg and up through the hole on the other leg. Knot the string, leaving 3 inches between the legs (see diagram). Cut off the extra string.

9 Cut a 15-inch length of string for the pull cord. Tie one end to the center of the arm string, then tie the string to the center of the leg string. Fold up the end and knot to make a loop at the end of the pull cord. Test-pull the cord. The arms and the legs will rise and fall as you pull the cord.

JUMPING JACK

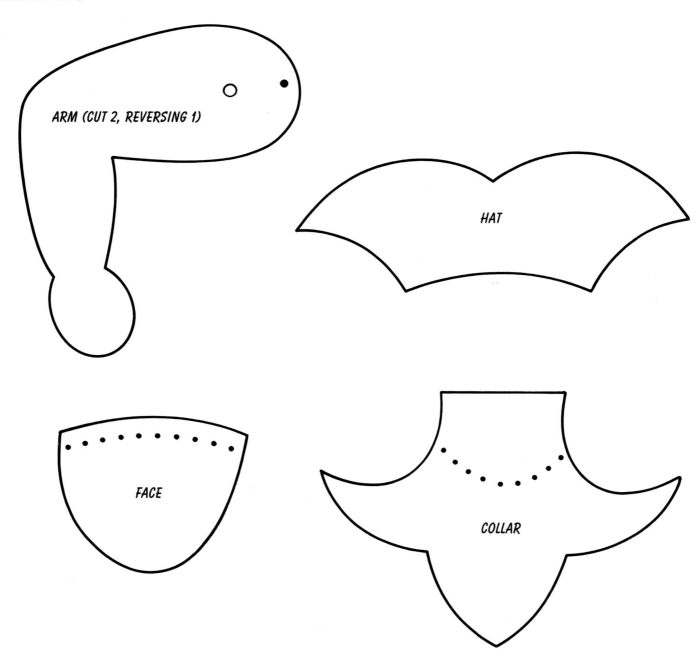

ARM (CUT 2, REVERSING 1)

HAT

FACE

COLLAR

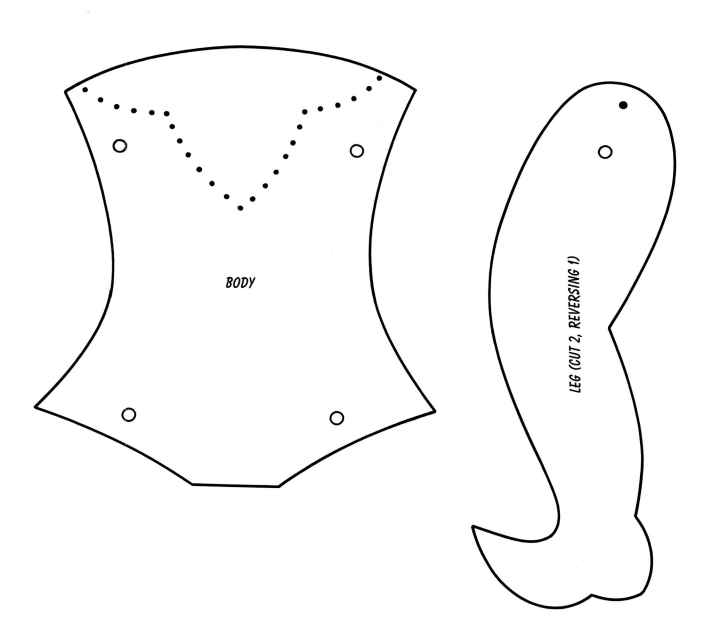

BODY

LEG (CUT 2, REVERSING 1)

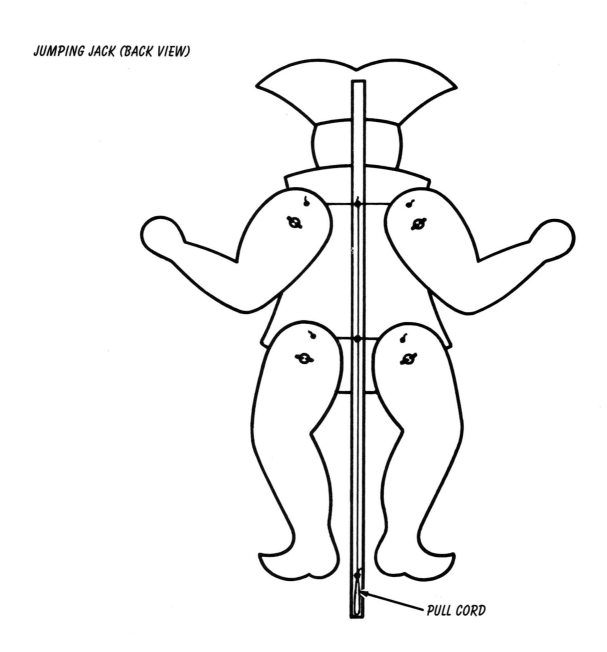

PULL CORD

TINY SPOOL DOLLS

INTERMEDIATE

Stylish as can be. One wears a button hat, the other has rainbow hair.

You will need:

Empty white spools from sewing thread
Scraps of fabric or ribbon in various colors
Pipe cleaners
Scraps of colorful yarn
Small round beads for nose
Button with shank for hat (optional)
Black felt-tipped marker
White glue
Blunt scissors
½-inch-wide paintbrush
Cotton swabs

1 Cut the cloth in a strip to fit the bottom two-thirds of the spool. Then with a cotton swab or brush, apply glue to the bottom two-thirds of the spool. Wrap the strip of cloth or a ribbon around the spool, leaving the top third of the spool uncovered for the face. Cut off any extra cloth.

2 Cut a 4½-inch length of pipe cleaner. Bend the piece around the back of the spool above the fabric. Glue the pipe cleaner in place and tape down. When the glue dries, remove the tape, then bend the arms outward and form the hands by bending the tips.

3 Draw on the dot eyes with the marker. Glue on the bead nose, holding the bead in place on the spool for a few minutes until the glue sets.

4 For pigtails, cut nine 5-inch strands of yarn. Tie the strands together at one end. Separate the strands into three groups of three strands each and braid together (see "How to Braid," page 163). Tie the strands together at the end to hold the braid. You can fluff out the yarn if you don't want to braid. Insert the knotted end into the hole of the spool.

STRETCHABLE CROCODILE AND CLOWN

EXPERIENCED

These funny figures are put together with Popsicle sticks and paper fasteners. Squeeze the "legs" together and the head shoots upward.

For both, you will need:

About fifty 6-inch-long super-size craft sticks or tongue depressors

About fifty 1-inch to 1½-inch paper fasteners

Press-on notebook reinforcement rings

Movable doll eyes

Two small black buttons

White glue

Acrylic paint in various colors

½-inch paintbrush

Drill with fine bit

Ruler

Craft knife

Rubber band or masking tape

Scrap of construction paper or poster board

NOTE: As this project requires use of a drill and a craft knife, it should not be attempted without an adult's help and supervision.

1 Mark a small hole centered ½ inch in from each end of several craft sticks.

2 For the body, stack groups of three or four craft sticks with a marked one on top. Hold stacks together with a rubber band or masking tape, and drill holes at marks through the stack.

3 For the arms, legs, and heads, drill a hole through one end only.

4 For each toy, cut two sticks to 3½-inch length for the top of the body. Drill a hole at each end.

5 For the crocodile, paint the sticks. Paint a row of triangles on one jaw. Glue eyes to the other jaw.

6 For the clown, glue three sticks edge to edge for the head (the center one has a hole at what would be the neck). From the construction paper or poster board, cut out a nose shaped like a teardrop, and from a scrap of stick also cut a little piece to place underneath the nose, to raise it. Glue the little piece to the teardrop and then the whole thing to the face. Glue the black button eyes in place. Paint the sticks, adding the hat, eyebrows, eyes, nose, and mouth as shown in the picture.

7 To put the toys together, line up the holes on two sticks and press the paper reinforcement rings onto the top stick. From the bottom up, insert a fastener at one end and flatten the ends over the ring (the ring side is the back of the toy). Follow the picture to put the toys together.

8 Press the bottom stick handles together and watch the crocodile and clown expand.

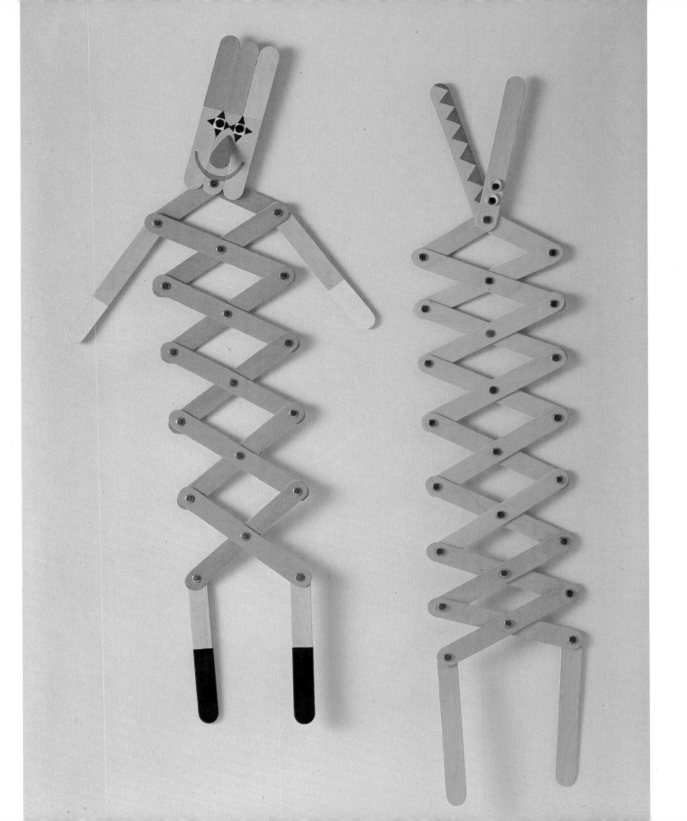

MAKE IT NATURALLY

TICK-TACK-TOE GAME

BEGINNER

An old favorite put together with flat stones. Paint with gaily colored O's and X's and you're set to play, indoors or out.

You will need:

9- to 12-inch-square slab of slate or scrap of wooden board painted gray

Ten small flat stones

Acrylic paints in two or more colors

¼-inch paintbrush

1 Place the smoother flat side of the slate slab (or board) right side up.

2 Dip the paintbrush into paint and draw two lines across the slate (or board) and two lines up and down to make the tick-tack-toe board.

3 With one color of paint, draw an X on each of five stones. With another color, draw a circle on each of the remaining five stones.

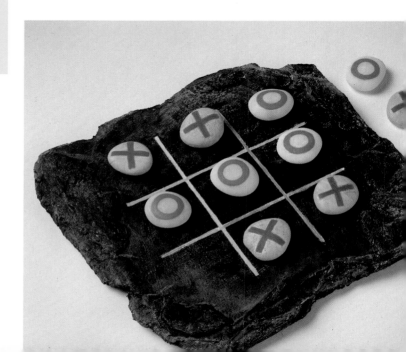

40

Rock Village

Half the fun is collecting rocks the right size and shape to make little houses and bushes and trees. The other half is playing decorator when you paint them.

You will need:

Large flat rocks or slabs of broken
    concrete with straight bottoms
    and slanted or shaped tops
    (ours are about 1 inch thick, 6
    to 8 inches wide, and 7 to 8
    inches high)
Small stone slabs or wooden boards
    for people, tree trunks, and
    support stands
Small rounded rocks for bushes
Flat pebbles for heads and treetops
Acrylic paints
Paintbrushes
Tacky glue

1 Wash the stones clean and let them dry.

2 For houses, stand the slabs upright, holding them in place by putting small pieces of wood or rocks in back of each house so it can stand by itself. You may have to try different-size supports in different positions until you find ones that hold the slabs upright. Glue the supports in place. Let the glue dry.

3 Paint the houses yellow, pink, tan, or any colors you like. Let each color dry before you add the next. Add roofs, doors, windows, bushes, and a heart like the one above the door on the left house in our picture.

4 Paint small rocks green for the bushes.

5 For the trees and any people, stand small slabs upright. Add support stones or wood scraps to the back as needed to make them stand up. Then glue flat pebbles on top of the slabs to make heads or treetops. Let the glue dry. Paint them as you wish.

Shell Pins and Magnets

Googly-eyed pins for a jacket or magnets for Mom's refrigerator, made from finds at the beach that are glued to scrap wood.

You will need:

Seashells, some about 2 to 3 inches
long for faces and some tiny
ones for noses
Small glue-on movable eyes
Small wood scraps (such as balsa or
pine)
Pin backs or magnets (available at
crafts supply stores)
White glue
Household cement
Paper towel

1 Wash shells and dry with a paper towel.

2 If the shell has a pointed end, use it for a nose or, using white glue, attach a tiny shell for the nose as shown on the scallop shell in our picture. Apply glue to the eyes and to the shell, holding the eyes in place until the glue is dry.

3 If your shell is hollow in back, fill in the hollow with scraps of wood, gluing them to make a flat area for the pin back or magnet.

4 With an adult's help, use the household cement to glue the pin back or magnet to the flat area on the back of the shell. You may need to hold the pin back or magnet in place with your fingers until the glue sets. Let the glue dry completely.

SHELL CATCHALL

A nice big clam shell is a perfect holder for clips or pins, especially when it is painted with a sailing ship or other picture recalling lazy vacation days.

You will need:

Large clam shell (ours was about 5½ inches across)
Small amount of sand
Acrylic paints
Paintbrush
White glue
Pencil

1 Wash the shell clean, and dry.

2 With a pencil, draw a boat or other beach scene on the inside of the shell.

3 Paint the scene, letting each color dry before adding the next.

4 Cover the beach area of your scene with glue and sprinkle on a coating of sand. Let the glue dry, then gently shake off any loose sand.

5 Use the shell for holding pocket change, paper clips, and so on.

TERRARIUM

EXPERIENCED

Bring the garden inside with a little glass-enclosed world of plants that grow all year round. A grand way to learn about plants and how they grow.

You will need:

Large fish bowl or other large
rounded glass container with a
wide enough opening for your
hands to fit through
Plastic wrap or a plastic plate big
enough to cover the bowl
opening (optional)
Small plants (see "Tips for a
Successful Terrarium," page 49)
Potting soil (porous, with perlite
particles)
Gravel (from pet fish store)
Charcoal barbecue briquette, or
charcoal for fish tank filters
Decorative trims (see "Tips for a
Successful Terrarium")

1 Clean the glass container, making sure to rinse off all soap and household cleaners.

2 Build a soil layer to fill up a quarter of the bowl's height as follows: Cover the bottom of the bowl with 1 inch of gravel. Crumble the charcoal briquette and spread a thin (about ¼-inch) layer of charcoal bits over the gravel. Add 2 inches or more of potting soil. Add mounds of soil to make your landscape more interesting.

3 Plan how you want to place your plants. If your terrarium will sit on a shelf to be seen from only one side, the tall plants should go at the back, with lower plants in the front. If the terrarium will sit on a table to be seen from all sides, place the tall plants in the middle with lower plants all around.

4 Beginning with the tallest plants, poke or dig a small hole for the roots. Keeping some of each plant's original soil on the roots, place the roots in the hole, then cover them with soil. Add the remaining plants, using different kinds of plants for variety.

5 Water the soil, dampening it completely but being careful not to overwater. Cover the opening with the plastic wrap or plate, if you wish.

6 Set the terrarium in a shady spot for several days to give the plants a chance to adjust to their new home and grow new roots.

7 Move the terrarium to a spot where it will get the right light for your plants.

8 Watch your terrarium. At night, moisture from the plants should collect on the bowl and slowly slide down the sides to keep the soil damp. If the moisture balance is just right, the terrarium can go for months or even years without needing more water. Once you have a good moisture balance, if you keep your container closed, lift the lid once a week to allow fresh air to enter.

9 If, however, you notice that the soil is dry, add a small amount of water. If too much moisture collects on the bowl during the day, if you see water standing in the bottom of the bowl, or if you see mold or mildew, remove the lid and leave it off to let the bowl dry out. Cover again after a few hours. As you watch your terrarium, you will learn what your special landscape needs to keep it healthy.

TIPS FOR A SUCCESSFUL TERRARIUM

A terrarium is a glass-contained little world whose plants can thrive with very little care. You can make your own little woodland using ferns and mosses, a miniature garden with flowering plants, or a desert with cactus plants.

Choosing plants: Decide what type of landscape you want and choose plants that need the same temperature, moisture, and amount of sunlight. Pick plants small enough to fit your bowl, whether you collect them outdoors, grow them from seed, or buy them at a store. Use different types of plants: tall or short, different colors or shapes of leaves, and so on.

Types of plants: Some of the plants that grow well in a terrarium are: coleus, small ferns, mosses, dwarf evergreens, grape ivy, African violets, miniature begonias, low-growing members of the Pilea and Peperomia families, and various cactus plants.

Decorative trims: You can make your terrarium more attractive by adding small rocks, paths of redwood chips or gravel, or even a small plastic or ceramic animal or gnome.

SHELL AND POMPON SNAKE

Puff, the stylish shell snake, is a friendly addition to any playroom. Put him together with pompons and small clamshells. You can make him a playmate if you like, strung together with other shells.

You will need:

Pair of mussel shells

Fifteen to twenty jingle shells (small, thin shells, ⅝ inch to 1 inch in diameter)

Pompons or beads in assorted colors and sizes (½ inch to ¾ inch in diameter)

Small glue-on movable eyes

Scrap of red felt

Heavy-duty thread

Needle

T-pin or thin nail

Blunt scissors

1 Separate the mussel shells if they are attached to each other. Wash the shells and let them dry.

2 With a T-pin or a nail, punch a hole in the center of each jingle shell. (If you are using shells that are too thick to punch a hole through, have an adult drill a hole with a fine bit.)

3 Cut an 18-inch-long piece of thread. Thread the needle with it and knot one end. Start at the tail with the smallest pompons and shells to thread first a pompon, then a shell, then another pompon and shell, and so on, using larger pompons and shells as you work up to the head.

4 When your snake is long enough, end with a pompon. Knot the thread just above the last pompon. Cut off the extra thread, leaving about 2 inches above the knot. Glue the thread end along the center on the inside of one mussel shell. That will become the lower jaw of the snake.

5 Cut a ½-inch by 2-inch strip of red felt. Cut a V out of one end to make a forked tongue. Glue the other end of the tongue to the inside of the mussel shell for the lower jaw, covering the thread end.

6 For the top of the snake's head, fit the narrow end of the second shell over the end of the shell with the tongue. Fit them together to make an open mouth as the picture shows. Glue the ends of the shells in place. Glue on the eyes.

NOTE: You can make any number of different snakes following this procedure. We've included one variation in our picture, using a cowrie shell for the snake's head.

Sand Sunburst

INTERMEDIATE

Souvenir of a sunny day at the beach, Smiley is just damp sand poured into a disposable pie plate, then solidified with plaster of Paris. A nice gift for a favorite grownup.

You will need:

Plaster of Paris (available at hardware and paint stores, or home centers)
Marbles or beads
Damp sand
Aluminum-foil pie pan
Plastic spoon

1 Pour some damp sand into the pie pan. Spread the sand out evenly to cover the whole bottom of the pan, using enough sand to make a layer about ½ inch deep.

2 With your fingers, press ridges, holes, or other designs into the top of the sand. Always keep at least a thin layer of sand covering the bottom of the pan. Add marbles or beads as you wish.

3 Mix the plaster of Paris following the directions on the package. (The mixture will be somewhat thin.) Spoon some plaster into the ridges and holes of your design. Then gently pour in a layer of plaster about ½ inch thick. Let the plaster dry completely (about an hour).

4 Turn the plate over to remove the casting, being careful not to let it drop. Some sand will stick to the plaster casting; carefully brush off any excess sand with your hands.

SAND CASTLE PENCIL HOLDER

This three-tower complex is assembled from toilet paper rolls, sand-coated to produce an imaginative container for pencils.

You will need:

> Three cardboard rolls from toilet
>   tissue
> Flat rock
> Black poster paint
> Sand
> Paper plate
> White glue
> Paintbrush
> Blunt scissors

1 Cut one roll to 3½ inches high. Cut small notches around one end of all three rolls, like those in the picture. Space them evenly.

2 Paint small square windows on the two taller rolls and a door on the short roll. Let the paint dry.

3 Place some sand on the paper plate.

4 With a paintbrush, cover the inside and the unpainted area on the outside of one roll with glue.

5 While the glue is still wet, roll the tube gently in the sand until it is covered completely. With your fingers, sprinkle sand to cover the inside of the tube.

6 Repeat for the other tubes. Let them dry.

7 Stand the tubes up, side by side, on the flat rock. Glue the bottom ends of the tubes to the rock. Pour a little puddle of glue inside the tubes to help hold them to the rock. Let the glue dry completely before using the holder.

Birds in Branches

EXPERIENCED

Fuzzy-headed little birds with polka-dotted nutshell bodies sit on a branch that could decorate a hallway.

You will need:

Small branches
Vase
Almonds in the shell
Brightly colored pompons
Colored pipe cleaners
Yellow seed beads
Round toothpicks
Acrylic paints in various colors
One ¼-inch-wide paintbrush
One fine paintbrush
White glue
Tape
Blunt scissors

1 Paint one side of an almond shell for each bird's back with the ¼" brush. With the fine brush, add small white dots to speckle the painted shell.

2 Apply glue to the wide end of the shell and attach a pompon head.

3 Bend a 3-inch piece of pipe cleaner in half. Then apply glue to the bottom of the shell, and on this glued area place the folded pipe cleaner with the ends facing the head. Hold in place with tape. When the glue is dry, remove the tape.

4 Paint each end of several toothpicks with yellow paint; let them dry. With scissors, snip off the painted tips and glue the cut edge of each tip into a pompon head for a beak. To make the eyes, put glue on the yellow seed beads and place two beads on each pompon.

5 Place the branches in a vase or other container. Curl the pipe-cleaner legs around the branches to perch the birds.

WHAT SHALL I DO TODAY?

SHADOW DRAWING

BEGINNER

Two can play at this game; so can a houseful of children. And it takes no special equipment of any kind—just sunshine or a good light.

You will need:

Large sheets of paper or a wide roll of brown wrapping paper (or even a sidewalk)
Crayons, chalk, or poster paints with paintbrushes
Pencil
Bright sunshine (outdoors) or bright light (indoors)

1 Stand facing the light so your shadow falls onto a large sheet of paper (or the sidewalk).

2 Try standing with your feet apart and your arms away from your body, moving as you need to in order to get a good (or funny) shadow. Then hold very still while you have a friend trace your shadow outline, using a pencil on paper or chalk on cement.

3 Draw in your face and clothes. Color or paint as you wish.

TIP: Make shadow drawings outdoors at different times of the day and see how your shadow changes as the sun is higher or lower in the sky.

WIND SOCK

EXPERIENCED

A breeze to make! Simply glue a fabric tube, hearts, and streamers to a plastic ring, and let her blow!

You will need:

15-inch by 23-inch piece of cotton-blend cloth
Scrap of cloth in contrasting color for hearts
15 yards of 1-inch-wide ribbon (or strips of fabric)
1 yard of narrow ribbon to match the wind sock fabric
7-inch-diameter metal, wooden, or plastic ring (available at crafts supply stores)
Small plastic curtain ring
Tacky glue
Tracing paper
Large-eyed needle
Blunt scissors
Iron

1 Get an adult to turn under 1 inch of fabric along each long edge of the cotton rectangle and press the fold under for a hem. Open the fold along one edge and apply glue to the inside edge, then fold over again on the iron line, creating the hem at the lower edge of the wind sock.

2 Trace the heart pattern below (see "How to Trace and Use Your Patterns," page 163). Cut five hearts from the cloth scrap. Apply glue to the hearts and place them on the right side of the large piece of cloth, spacing them evenly across the center, starting and ending about 1¼ inches in from the side edges.

3 Cut the wider ribbon into twenty-two streamers each 24 inches long.

HEART PATTERN

4 With the wrong side of the cloth and the streamers facing you, start ⅞ inch in from one side edge to glue the streamers in place. Apply glue to 1 inch of the end of each streamer, placing these 1-inch ends side by side over the entire length of the lower hem. Let the glue dry for a couple of hours.

5 With the hearts on the outside, place the cloth around the large ring to make sure it fits. Overlap the side edges and glue them together to form a tube. Let the glue dry.

6 Glue the top hem over the large ring.

7 Cut the narrow ribbon into thirds. Thread a ribbon through the large-eyed needle. Poke the needle through the top hem. Knot one end of the ribbon around the ring edge. Thread and knot the other two ribbons evenly spaced around the top edge.

8 Knot the free ends of the narrow ribbons together around the curtain ring for a hanging loop.

WATER SCOPE

Want to see what goes on under water in a tidal pool? A can, a rubber band, and plastic wrap combine to provide a view.

You will need:

Empty fruit juice or coffee can
Plastic kitchen wrap
Rubber bands (to fit tightly around
   the can)
Plastic tape
Can opener

1 Carefully remove both ends from the can with the can opener. (To minimize risk of getting cut on the sharp edges, it may be better to have an adult do this.)

2 Stretch a piece of plastic wrap over one end of the can. Hold it tightly in place with one or more rubber bands. Pull the wrap tight so it covers the end of the can without any wrinkles. Trim away the extra plastic wrap and cover the edge all around with plastic tape.

3 Use the water scope in shallow wading water, pressing the plastic-covered end of the can down into the water several inches (but not up to the top) to see objects on the bottom more clearly.

Pretend Beach Sailboat

BEGINNER

It won't survive high tide, but will sail wherever imagination takes it. All you need are two sticks, a piece of sheeting . . . and a beach.

You will need:

Old sheet or 1 yard of scrap material
   (enough for two sails)
Two sticks—one about 4 feet long,
   another about 1½ feet long
Blunt scissors

1 Cut or tear the fabric to make a 36-inch square. Fold the square diagonally to make a triangle. Cut along the fold to make two sails.

2 Dig out a boat-shaped hollow area in the beach sand for the boat hull. For the mast, plant one end of the long stick in the sand within the hull, placing it toward the front (bow) end of the hull area.

3 Tie one corner of the sail (use the corner opposite the long diagonal side of the sail) to the bottom of the mast.

4 Tie another point of the sail to the top of the mast.

5 Have a friend hold the mast firmly to keep it upright while you stretch out the remaining point of the sail toward the back (stern) end of the boat. "Plant" the short stick in the sand at the stern and tie the last point of the sail to it.

6 Climb aboard, mate, and sail as far as your imagination allows. When it's time to leave the beach, take your sail and sticks with you to leave the beach clean and have your sail ready for your next beach trip.

PEA AND TOOTHPICK CREATION

INTERMEDIATE

This provides hours of indoor play, with toothpicks and dried peas softened to serve as connectors.

You will need:

> Round toothpicks
> Large round dried peas
> White glue

8 TOOTHPICKS

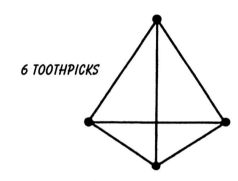

6 TOOTHPICKS

BASE DIAGRAMS

1 Soak the peas in a bowl of hot tap water for about four hours to soften.

2 Following one of the diagrams, make a base by dipping the tips of the toothpicks into glue, then sticking the tips into the peas.

3 Keep sticking peas and toothpicks together, adding onto the base to build a structure of squares and triangles. Let the structure dry.

4 The peas will shrink during drying, and you may need to add more glue to some toothpicks and stick them into the peas again.

PUFF-PAINT SNEAKERS

BEGINNER

Turn plain white sneakers into 3-D marvels by squeezing puff paint on them.

You will need:

Sneakers
Puff paint in assorted colors
    (available at crafts supply stores)
Soft pencil

1 Lightly pencil a design of your own onto the sneakers or, following the picture, draw a sun, trees, and clouds.

2 Following the directions on the paint tube, squeeze puff paint along the seams of the sneaker and along your pencil lines. Let the paint dry. Do not iron the sneakers; the paint will dry in raised lines.

PUFF-PAINT SWEATSHIRT

BEGINNER

Scribble and dribble to your heart's content, and then wear your own "exclusive" design wherever you go.

You will need:

Sweatshirt
Puff paint in assorted colors
    (available at crafts supply stores)
Soft pencil
Iron

1 Lightly pencil a design of your own, or follow the picture and draw stars, hearts, spirals, circles, squiggles, or other shapes all over the front of the sweatshirt.

2 Squeeze puff paint along your pencil lines.

3 After the paint has dried (in six to eight hours), have an adult iron the shirt, following the directions on the paint tube (or that came with the tube) to make the paint lines puff up. (They will puff some as they dry; ironing will give you a fuller effect.)

BEAN NECKLACE

INTERMEDIATE

Raid the family sewing box for the button necklace . . . and make a matching barrette, as well. Or soak some dried beans until they're soft enough to string, and look— another crafty necklace!

You will need:

Assorted dried beans (such as
    kidney, lima, navy, or chickpeas)
1 yard nylon monofilament thread
    (available at crafts supply stores)
Sewing needle
Waxed paper
Blunt scissors

1 Soak the beans overnight in cold tap water to soften.

2 Thread the thread through the needle. Drain the beans. Thread the beans onto the thread, poking the needle through the center of each bean, alternating the types of beans as you thread them. Keep stringing the beans onto the thread for several inches more than you need for your necklace, because the beans will shrink as they dry. (Lima beans may also split as they dry, forming interesting shapes.)

3 Let the necklace dry on waxed paper.

4 When the beans are dry and firm to the touch, gently slide them close together along the thread. Knot the two ends of the thread together at the length you want. Cut off any extra thread 1 inch beyond the knot.

NOTE: The Bean Necklace is shown worn at left in our photograph here and on page 72.

Button Necklace and Barrette

INTERMEDIATE

You will need:

About forty 4-hole buttons, 7/8 inch
    to 1⅛ inch diameter in white
    and various colors
Several yards of colored pearl
    cotton or string
Plain hair clip
Tacky glue or household cement
Tapestry needle that fits through
    holes in buttons
Blunt scissors

BUTTON NECKLACE

1 Thread the needle with string 1 yard long. (Use two strands that are each 1 yard long if you are working with thin string.)

2 Bring the needle up through one hole of the first button and down through the hole that is diagonally opposite (see diagram).

3 Continue to thread the buttons in this way, alternating white and colored buttons and overlapping the edges.

4 When the necklace is as long as you want it, knot the string ends together and cut off any extra string.

BUTTON BARRETTE

1 Thread the needle with ½ yard of string.

2 Bring the needle up through a hole in a larger button and down through the next hole beside it. Thread another, smaller button in the same way, overlapping the two button edges (see diagram).

3 Thread the string through the remaining two holes in the second button, then through the last two holes of the first button.

4 Tie the string ends securely together on the back of the buttons.

5 Glue the buttons to the hair clip.

NOTE: The button necklace and barrette are shown worn at right in our photographs.

BUTTON BARRETTE DIAGRAM

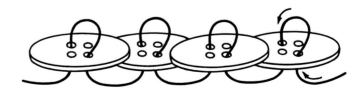

BUTTON NECKLACE DIAGRAM

SHELL AND FEATHER ANIMALS

See how our small sailor has transformed his gob's cap into a fantasy creation with figures made from shells and feathers.

You will need:

Gob's (sailor's) hat
Small whelk shells
Small colored marabou feathers
   (available in crafts supply stores)
Small glue-on movable eyes (also
   available in crafts supply stores)
Tacky glue
Sewing needle
Invisible thread (nylon monofilament,
   available in crafts supply stores)

1 Glue eyes and feathers onto each shell as you wish, letting the shape of each shell tell you how to decorate. For example, the pointed end on a shell may look like a nose. You can also glue on beads, small pompons, sprinkle on glitter, or add other trims to design your own creature.

2 Glue the decorated shells to the brim of the hat. With a needle and invisible thread, sew several tight loops over the shell to tack it securely in place. You may need to wear a thimble or get an adult's help to push the needle through the brim.

Tie-dyed T-Shirts

EXPERIENCED

Sure to be all the rage for all ages, but a project perhaps best suited to older children in the family.

You will need:

White 100-percent cotton T-shirts
8-ounce bottles of liquid dye (we used Rit blue, yellow, and bright pink)
¼-inch-wide rubber bands
10-quart dishpan or pail (plastic may become stained; use enameled pails if you wish). Two pans are needed for the pink and yellow T-shirt.
Rubber gloves
Plastic drop cloth
White paper towels
Newspapers

Before you begin: Wash and dry the T-shirts. Protect your hands with rubber gloves when dyeing. Remove any rugs from the workplace and use drop cloth to protect both the floor and work surfaces.

Blue T-Shirt

1 Starting at the bottom edge, make 2-inch-deep accordion folds across the T-shirt, working up to the neck. Fold the sleeves in toward the neck (see Diagram 1).

2 Wrap five evenly spaced rubber bands several times each around the folded layers. (The dye will not color the fabric at the rubber bands.)

3 Add the bottle of blue dye to a dishpan containing 6 to 8 quarts of hot tap water. Place the T-shirt in the dye bath and soak for ten minutes.

4 Remove the T-shirt from the dye bath and rinse it in cool water until the water runs clear. Gently squeeze out as much water as you can.

5 Place the shirt on newspapers covered with white paper towels to absorb the moisture. Replace the papers when they become soaked.

6 When the T-shirt is damp dry, remove the rubber bands. You can finish drying the shirt in the dryer or by ironing it.

DIAGRAM 1

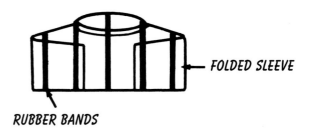

FOLDED SLEEVE

RUBBER BANDS

PINK AND YELLOW T-SHIRT

1 Starting at one lower corner, make accordion pleats every 2 inches diagonally across the T-shirt (see Diagram 2). Fold the sleeves in toward the neck.

2 Wrap five evenly spaced rubber bands several times each around the folded layers.

3 Add 6 to 8 quarts of hot tap water to each of two dishpans. Add the bottle of pink dye to one dishpan, yellow dye to the other.

4 Dip half the T-shirt in the yellow dye bath, holding it in place for seven minutes. Then remove the shirt and dip the other half in the pink bath for three minutes. (Where the yellow half and the pink half overlap, the shirt will turn orange.)

5 Then rinse the shirt in the sink in cool water, *holding one half out of the water while you rinse the other half,* to rinse the colors separately. Do this until the water runs clear. Gently squeeze out as much water as you can.

6 Place the shirt on newspapers covered with white paper towels to absorb the moisture. Replace the papers when they become soaked.

7 When the T-shirt is damp dry, remove the rubber bands. You can finish drying the shirt in the dryer or by ironing it.

DIAGRAM 2

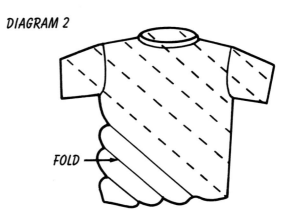

FOLD →

DINOSAUR PINS

Paint your favorite animal cracker figures to create a bright new decoration for a T-shirt or lapel.

You will need:

Animal crackers (we used Salerno®
  Dinosaur Grrrahams™ graham
  cookies, available at
  supermarkets)
Acrylic paints
Two paintbrushes
Black felt-tipped marker
Pin backs (available at crafts supply
  stores)
Tacky glue
Mod Podge®

1 Paint the back of each cookie or cracker; let it dry.

2 Paint the front and edges of the cookies or crackers, making sure that you cover each one completely. Let the paint dry. Then paint a second coat and let it dry.

3 With the marker, draw a mouth and eye on each animal.

4 With a clean paintbrush, apply one or more coats of Mod Podge to the painted cookie or cracker, letting it dry completely after each coat.

5 Glue the flat surface of a pin back to the upper portion of the cookie or cracker back. Let the glue dry completely.

DESK SET

BEGINNER

Postage stamps decorate a box and a can to hold stationery and pencils.

You will need:

Used postage stamps
Cigar box, tin can, or other container to be covered
Waxed paper
White glue
Sponge

1 To prepare used stamps, soak the stamps off envelopes by placing them in cold water until they float loose. Dry the stamps face down on waxed paper, lifting and moving them occasionally to hasten drying. (Stamps may curl as they dry, but they will flatten when glued.)

2 Glue the backs of the stamps and attach them to the box or can, overlapping the edges and covering the entire surface of the container. With a damp sponge, wipe away any glue that oozes out as you are working. Let the glue dry.

PAPERWEIGHTS

A fantastic use of old jars to display weird animals and foliage (or any found objects that a child takes a fancy to).

You will need:

> Jars with tight-fitting lids, 8- to 12-ounce size
> Florist's clay
> Small plastic figures, animals, and plants (from a variety or toy store; plastic plants are also available in fish or pet stores)

1 Clean the jars and lids thoroughly with soap and water. Dry them completely.

2 Place the jar lids with the flat side down and the rim up on your worktable. Press some clay into each jar lid, covering the lid out to the rim and mounding the clay slightly at the center.

3 Poke the stem or bottom of a plant into the center of the clay, pressing the clay tightly around the stem to hold it securely in place. Try fitting the jar over the plant. If the plant is too tall or bushy, neatly trim the top or the ends of the leaves to make it fit within the jar.

4 Arrange the animals and figures around the plant, pressing the clay around their feet. Add more plants if you wish.

5 Place the jar in the sink and fill it almost to the brim with water.

6 Carefully turn the lid with the figures upside down. Insert the figures into the jar of water, then screw the lid on very tightly.

7 Wipe the outside of the jar dry and turn it upside down with the lid at the bottom for your paperweight.

NOTE: You can also design your own scenes, using plastic flowers, marbles, seashells, or small ceramic figures.

STRING PICTURE

Picture-making with yarn strung at random and in colors to please a child's sense of decor.

You will need:

A wooden board (we used a 12-inch square of ¾-inch plywood)
1-inch-long common nails
String, metallic gift cord, and scrap yarn in various colors
Ruler
Pencil
Hammer
Sandpaper
Sawtooth hanger (optional)

1 Sand the edges of the board.

2 Measure and draw a line all around the square ¾ inch in from the edge.

3 Hammer in nails scattered along the line and within the square. Nails should be driven in so they don't wobble, but with at least ½ inch remaining above the board.

4 Tie a string to one nail, then loop the string rather tightly from nail to nail as you wish all over the square, tying on new colors of string or yarn as desired. When the board is well covered, tie the string end to a nail.

5 Tuck all the knots into the work to hide them.

6 If you wish, attach a sawtooth hanger to the back of the board to hang your picture.

Soap Dish

EXPERIENCED

An outlined hand cut from air-drying clay holds soap at the ready for whenever the crafter's hands and face need washing.

You will need:

Air-drying clay (available at hobby, art supply, and variety stores)
Acrylic paints in various colors
1-inch paintbrush
Rolling pin
Toothpicks
Dinner knife
Small textured object such as washable costume jewelry for imprinting design (optional)

1 Roll out some clay to make a ¼-inch-thick slab bigger than your hand.

2 Place your hand over the center of the clay slab and trace all around your hand with a toothpick. With a dinner knife, cut out the hand shape, following the outline made by the toothpick.

3 If you wish, press the textured object into the center of the palm, or draw your own design with a toothpick. (Be sure to wash the jewelry or other object clean before any clay dries on it.) Poke small drainage holes through the clay at the center of your design.

4 Bend the clay to shape the hand, pushing up the edges along the thumb and the little finger, or curling the fingers as shown. Prop the hand against bottles or any other handy objects to hold its shape. Let the clay dry completely.

5 Paint the hand soap dish with two or more coats of acrylic paint to waterproof it. Then paint the design area in a contrasting color, if you wish, letting each coat of paint dry completely before adding the next.

NOTE: A soap dish made with fingers slightly spread will allow air to circulate around the bar of soap, and avoid soap waste.

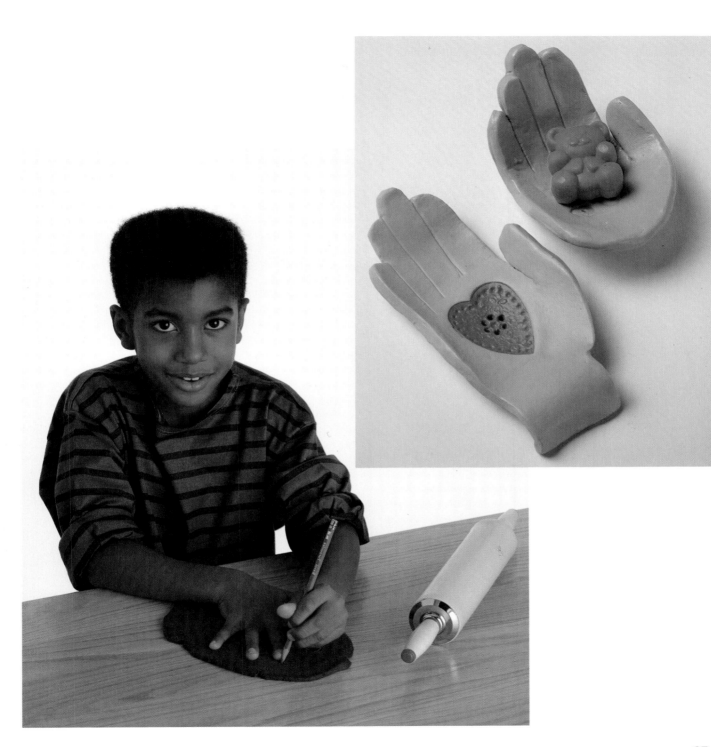

LEAF RUBBING

BEGINNER

A sure way to bring out any child's artistic soul—rubbing over found objects to create pictures with a textured feeling.

You will need:

Leaves
Nonerasable white typing paper
Crayons
9-inch by 12-inch construction paper
    of any color
White glue

1 You can arrange your leaves first or plan where to place them as you work.

2 Place a leaf under the white typing paper. Without moving the paper, rub a crayon on the paper over the leaf. Color over the whole leaf, but try not to go beyond the edges.

3 Make several more rubbings on the same sheet (some can be at the edge of the paper) until you have a nice design.

4 Apply glue to the corners on the back of the leaf paper and press onto the construction paper, leaving an even border all around.

Sponge-Print Wrapping Paper

BEGINNER

Plain brown paper isn't plain anymore after sponge printing. It's great wrapping for any kind of present, and making it provides satisfaction for any crafts beginner.

You will need:

Roll of brown wrapping paper
Cellulose household sponge
Poster paints
White paper towels
Blunt scissors
Aluminum-foil pie plates or shallow
    pans
Scrap paper

1 Cut the sponge into small shapes such as circles, hearts, squares, triangles, or strips (for printing stripes). Cut a separate piece of sponge for each shape in each color you plan to use.

2 Using a separate dish for each color, pour a small puddle of paint into each pie plate or pan.

3 Dip the sponge into the paint, then blot off any extra paint on paper towels. Press the paint-covered surface of the sponge onto some scrap paper for practice and lift the sponge straight up to avoid smearing the paint. Practice until you can make good prints with just the right amount of paint on the sponge and without smearing the designs.

4 Unroll several feet of the wrapping paper on a flat worktable.

5 Print designs on the wrapping paper, scattering the shapes all over the paper or making a regular design, as you wish. To print stripes, use a narrow strip of the sponge. Press it down as many times as necessary to make a continuous, long stripe, overlapping the impressions to avoid any breaks in color.

ERASER-PRINT STATIONERY

INTERMEDIATE

Hearts and stars and various geometric shapes create lively notecards for a child's correspondence.

You will need:

Letter paper and notecards
Pink oblong rubber erasers
Pencils with erasers
Flat erasers in different shapes
Rubber eraser caps for pencils
Ink pads in one or more colors
Craft knife
Scrap paper

1 For a triangle shape, have an adult use the craft knife to cut off the end of a pink oblong eraser. Use the triangular-shaped side edge for a stamp.

2 Have a square about ⅝ inch across cut for a square stamp.

3 To make rings, stamp with the bottom end of the eraser cap.

4 Press the eraser stamps onto the ink pad and practice making designs on scrap paper until you can make neat, even prints.

5 Print your designs scattered or evenly spaced on the front of the notecards. Make a border across the top and along the left side of the letter paper, alternating colors and shapes as shown.

Found-Object Picture Rubbing

BEGINNER

You will need:

9-inch by 12-inch construction paper
White typing paper
Crayons
Assorted small flat objects with
   textured surfaces, such as coins,
   bits of upholstery, burlap, moiré
   and other textured fabrics, trims,
   grosgrain ribbon, rough-grained
   wood, zippers, and anything else
   you can find with interesting
   rough textures.

1 Place your object under a sheet of typing paper and rub a crayon over the object to make a rubbed design on the paper.

2 Practice with different objects until you find several that make rubbing designs you like.

3 You can work several ways to make your picture. You can arrange the objects as you wish to make an interesting design. Then place a fresh sheet of typing paper over the objects and make your rubbing, using one or more colors as you wish. You can also draw outlines (as for the house in our picture) and then rub, using different colors and textures for the different outlined shapes.

4 To mount your picture, dab glue on the back corners and attach the picture, centered, to a sheet of construction paper.

LEAF PRINTS

An enjoyable, instructive pastime, using acrylic paint and leaves to produce decorative designs on paper.

You will need:

Leaves

Plain notecards (or precut mat for a picture frame)

Acrylic paint in various colors

1-inch-wide paintbrush

Scrap paper

1 Lay a leaf flat on a covered work surface. Brush some paint onto the front of the leaf, then press the leaf, paint side down, onto a piece of scrap paper to make a print. Carefully lift the leaf up without smudging the paint. Practice on scrap paper until you can make good prints.

2 Print one or more leaf prints as you wish on the front of the notecards. Let the paint dry before handling.

NOTE: Leaf prints are also good for decorating gift wrap, picture mats, and paper place mats.

Fruit and Vegetable Prints

BEGINNER

Uniquely imaginative outfits result from stamping fabric with paint-laden apple cross-sections, orange slices, and other pieces of fruit or vegetables.

You will need:

Cotton-blend T-shirts and shorts
Fresh fruits or vegetables (we used
    apples, oranges, limes, star fruit,
    carrots, radishes, and flat parsley
    to make the radish "leaves")
Fabric paint in assorted bright colors
1-inch-wide paintbrush
White paper towels
Scrap paper
Waxed paper
Ironing board

1 Cut the fruits or vegetables in half to make cross-sections and, if you wish, cut orange wedges and carrot sticks.

2 Blot the cut surfaces well with paper towels to remove as much juice as you can.

3 Brush fabric paint onto the cut surface or onto the parsley leaves and practice printing on scrap paper until you can make good prints.

4 Use an ironing board as a work surface when you stamp. Place waxed paper on the ironing board to protect it, and cover it with a single layer of the cloth to be printed. Keep the part you are stamping flat, with waxed paper underneath, and stamp designs over the clothing as you wish.

FUN FOR SPECIAL OCCASIONS

HOW TO SAY I LOVE YOU

HEART STICKERS POT

BEGINNER

Stickers decorate a flower pot for a gift made with love to give a favorite grown-up.

You will need:

Small flowering plant
White plastic flower pot, slightly
    larger than plant's original pot
Red heart stickers
Potting soil

1 Cover the white pot with scattered stickers all around the outside.

2 If the decorated pot is deeper than the original pot, add some potting soil to the bottom of the white pot to raise the plant to its proper height.

3 With an adult's help, gently remove the plant from its old pot and place it into the new pot, adding extra soil as needed to fill in spaces around the edge of the pot.

4 Water the plant to dampen the new soil, adding more soil in any spots that settle as they become wet.

VALENTINE CROWN

Mom is the queen of the day, wearing a crown of cardboard, pipe cleaners, doilies, and heart stickers glued and stapled together by a little boy or girl who loves her.

You will need:

Red poster board
Pink construction paper
Three red and three white heart-
    shaped doilies, about 6 inches
    wide
Three gold heart-shaped doilies,
    about 4½ inches wide
Heart stickers
Pipe cleaners
Stapler
White glue
Tracing paper
Pencil
Blunt scissors

1 Cut a 4-inch by 24-inch strip of red poster board. Fit the strip around your head, overlapping the ends. Staple the overlapped ends together to hold the crown shape.

2 Trace the heart pattern (see "How to Trace and Use Your Patterns," page 163). Cut out the shape. Trace around the pattern to draw six hearts on the pink paper. Cut out the hearts. Cut the solid heart-shaped center from three red doilies.

3 Glue a pink heart to one end of two long pipe cleaners. Cut two other pipe cleaners in half, and glue a pink heart to one end of each half. Attach a sticker to the center of each heart.

4 Glue or staple the plain end of the two long pipe cleaners inside the center front of the crown. Glue or staple a pair of the short pipe cleaners to each side of the crown.

5 Glue three white doilies around the outside of the crown below the pink hearts on pipe cleaners. Glue a gold doily over each white doily. Glue on a red heart (the cut-out center of a red doily), then add a sticker to the center of each red heart.

HEART PATTERN

FOLDED-HANDS VALENTINE

BEGINNER

This greeting says "Be My Valentine," with the giver's own hand shape forming the card. An easy project for a beginning crafter.

You will need:

Pink, red, and white construction
  paper
Felt-tipped marker
White glue or glue stick
Tracing paper
Blunt scissors
Ruler
Pencil

1 Cut a 7-inch by 10-inch piece of pink construction paper. Fold it in half to form a card 5 inches by 7 inches.

2 Place your hand on the card with the little finger next to the fold. Separate your fingers slightly. With a pencil, lightly draw the outline of your hand on the card.

3 Cut out the hand shape, cutting through both layers of paper but without cutting along the folded edge.

4 Trace the heart patterns (see "How to Trace and Use Your Patterns," page 163) and cut out each shape. Using the patterns, cut out a large red heart and a smaller white heart.

5 Write a message on the white heart with the felt-tipped marker.

6 Fold the hearts in half (with the message inside the white heart). Glue the white heart centered on top of the red heart.

7 Glue the fold on the hearts to the inside fold line on the hands as shown.

HEART PATTERNS

HAND ME YOUR ♡

HANGING BASKET

BEGINNER

Paper plates ornamented with a child's choice of rubber stamps, stickers, crayons, or paint create this Valentine basket.

You will need:

Two white paper plates
Heart-shaped rubber stamps
    (optional)
Red ink pad (optional)
Bouquet of dried flowers
6 yards of narrow ribbon
White glue
Paper punch

1 Decorate the paper plates with heart stamps, following the border around the paper plate, or, if you prefer, draw your own design with markers or crayons, or decorate the plates with stickers.

2 Fold each plate in half with the design on the outside. Following the diagram, fit the edge of one folded plate inside the other to form a basket. Glue the overlapped edges together on each side of the basket, leaving an opening at the center.

3 With a paper punch, punch holes for handles as shown in the diagram.

4 Cut four 1½-yard lengths of ribbon. Thread the ends of two ribbons through the hole on each side, leaving about 18 inches for a handle. Wrap the center of each remaining ribbon back and forth to form loops; knot the handle-ribbon ends around these extra loops, and then tie the handle ends into a bow on each side as shown in the picture.

5 Fill the basket with the dried flowers.

HANGING BASKET

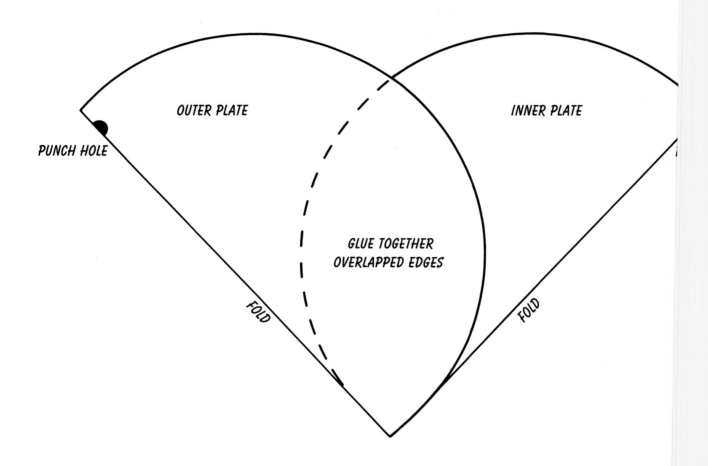

OUTER PLATE

INNER PLATE

PUNCH HOLE

GLUE TOGETHER
OVERLAPPED EDGES

FOLD

FOLD

LOVING CUP

BEGINNER

An easy project for any youngster in a gift-giving mood. Substitute "Mom" or "Grandpa" or any name on the child's list of favorite family members or friends for this personally crafted gift of love.

You will need:

Plain white coffee mug
Water-based enamel (such as Deka Gloss)
Small pointed paintbrush

1 Practice making letters on scrap paper until you can make neat letters with just the right amount of paint on the brush (enough to complete a stroke, but not so much that the paint smears).

2 Neatly paint "I LOVE DAD" (or, maybe, MOM or GRANDMA) on the mug.

3 Holding the mug by the handle as you work, so you don't touch the painted letters, paint hearts on the rest of the outside of the mug. Let the paint dry.

EASTER EGG-CITEMENT

SPONGE-PRINT EGGS

BEGINNER

A pretty token of spring, easy for a beginner to decorate and fun for parents and children to create together.

You will need:

Eggs
Egg-dyeing kit (we used Paas®
  Easter Egg Coloring Kit)
Household sponges
Nontoxic acrylic paints in various
  colors
Several small disposable aluminum-
  foil pans
White paper towels
Blunt scissors

1 Hard-cook the eggs (see "To Hard-C
ter Eggs," page 113).

2 Dye the hard-cooked eggs, if yc
while they are still warm, following d
on the color kit box.

3 From the sponges, cut small h
other simple shapes, such as circle
gles, or squares. Make a separa
sponge for each color you plan to use

4 Pour a small amount of paint
pans, using a separate pan for each c

5 Wet a sponge and squeeze out as r
ter as you can. Dip the damp sponge
paint color. Blot any excess paint or
towel to prevent dripping. Then press
egg to print your design. Allow the
dry between each color.

6 Repeat with other colors and
scattering the printed shapes ove
with or without overlapping them.

TO HARD-COOK EASTER EGGS . . .

This method helps you to avoid cracked shells and a dark rim around the yolk.

You will need:

Eggs
Large saucepan
Kitchen tongs

1 With an adult's help, place the eggs in the saucepan. Add enough cold water to cover the eggs, plus another inch. Bring the water to a full, rolling boil, then remove the pan from the heat. Cover the pan and let it stand, with the eggs still in the water, for twelve minutes.

2 Remove the eggs with tongs or a spoon and rinse them in cold water. The eggs are hard-cooked. Allow the eggs to dry thoroughly before dyeing or decorating them in any way.

3 Keep the eggs warm if you plan to dye them.

CRACKED-SHELL EGGS

EXPERIENCED

*This two-shell treatment creates a
challenging little puzzle for the crafter.*

You will need:

**Eggs
Egg-dyeing kit
Nontoxic tacky glue**

1 Hard-cook the eggs you plan
(see "To Hard-Cook Easter Eggs," p

2 Dye the hard-cooked eggs whi
still warm, following directions o
kit box.

3 Crack several raw eggs and e
into a bowl or cup (refrigerate and
cooking). Wash the eggshells cle
them dry.

4 Spread tacky glue over a small
dyed egg. Break off a piece of th
eggshell. (Use a piece from a par
the glued area so that the curves (
will match.) Press the piece of sh
dyed egg, cracking the piece into
as you do so. Slide the little pie(
leave small, even spaces between
bits. Allow the glue to dry thoroug

Glue other parts of the dyed eg
them with the shell pieces in th
until the whole egg is decorated.

STICKER EGGS

BEGINNER

Even the youngest member of the clan can add a favorite sticker to create a festive look.

You will need:

Eggs
Small, self-adhesive stickers and
  dots (available from stationery,
  gift, and party stores)
Teaspoon

1 Hard-cook the eggs (see "To Hard-Cook Easter Eggs," page 113).

2 Press stickers onto the eggs.

3 Rub over the stickers lightly with the back of the spoon to seal the edges tightly against the egg.

NOTE: The stickers may loosen if the eggs are refrigerated.

CANDY-COATED EGGS

BEGINNER

Here's a nice easy way to give three-dimensional interest to an egg's smooth exterior.

You will need:

Eggs
Sugar-dot baking decorations (such
    as Cake Mates' Snowflake Decors)
Nontoxic white glue
Small paintbrush
Small bowl

1 Hard-cook the eggs (see "To Ha[...]
ter Eggs," page 113).

2 Put the baking decorations i[...]
bowl.

3 Brush white glue over half an[...]
glued end into the bowl of decora[...]
it around to pick up candies. Pa[...]
tions in place so they lie flat aga[...]
Let the glue dry.

4 Finish the other half of th[...]
same way.

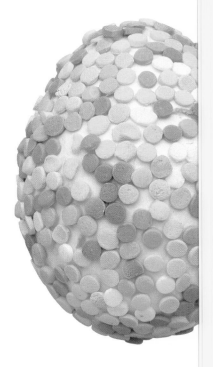

CRAYON-STRIPED EGGS

BEGINNER

It isn't magic . . . but it seems like it, when the dye colors the egg without touching the crayon stripes.

You will need:

Eggs
Egg-dyeing kit
Wax crayons or, for brighter colors, use Cray-pas (available in art supply stores)

1 Hard-cook the eggs (see "To Hard-Cook Easter Eggs," page 113).

2 With crayons, draw lines around each egg, leaving a little space between the bands as shown in the picture.

3 Dye the eggs, following instructions on the dye package, to create the solid-color background.

BREAD-DOUGH FLOWER EGGS

EXPERIENCED

Children who love to roll dough will enjoy this, but it could be tricky for some little hands.

You will need:

Eggs
Egg-dyeing kit
Slice of fresh white bread for each
    egg
Nontoxic acrylic paints in red and
    green
White glue
Tracing paper
Pencil
Waxed paper
Rolling pin
Cups
Tablespoon
Toothpick
Craft knife (optional)

1 Hard-cook the eggs (see "To F
ter Eggs," page 113).

2 Dye the eggs while they are
lowing directions on the color

3 Trace the tulip and leaf pat
paper (see "How to Trace and
terns," page 163). Cut out eac

4 Remove the crust from a
bread, then crumble the slice
one tablespoon of white glue
mix thoroughly. Knead (roll
your fingers) until it is smoo
crumbs or glue until the lum
like clay.

5 Divide the dough in half
cups for each color, mix a s
into the dough with your h
lump is colored all the way th

6 Now place the lumps of do
sheets of waxed paper, keepi
apart, and roll them out wit
until they are very thin.

7 Remove the top waxed paper and place the pattern shapes on the dough. With the tip of a toothpick, trace around the patterns on the dough. Carefully go around the outline once more, cutting all the way through the dough (or have an adult help cut out the shapes with a craft knife). Remove the excess dough.

8 Apply a little glue to the egg, then lift and gently press the dough shapes onto the egg, placing them as in the pattern. Let the glue dry.

TULIP PATTERN

SPECKLED EGGS

This is fun for a child enchanted with colors, and the result will be a happy addition to an Easter basket with plain dyed eggs.

You will need:

Eggs
Household sponge
Acrylic paints in various colors
Several small disposable aluminum-
    foil pans
Paper towels
Blunt Scissors

1 Hard-cook the eggs (see "? ter Eggs, page 113).

2 Cut small squares or sponge. Make a separate each color you plan to use.

3 Pour a small amount c pan, using a separate pan f

4 Wet a sponge and sque water. Dip the dampened paint color. Blot any exces towel, then print by pressir the sponge gently onto an e carefully to avoid smearin several prints scattered ov paint dry.

5 Repeat with other col overlapping the edges of tl egg is printed all over.

ASK

*...ners make the whiskers;
...nd a felt-and-paper nose
...form cheap eyeglass frames
...k.*

...unglasses with hard,
...nt frames (glue will not
...oft, opaque plastic)
...ible-ply bristol board

...arkers in various colors

...s

1 Remove the lenses from the sunglass frames by gently pushing them out.

2 Trace the nose pattern (see "How to Trace and Use Your Patterns," page 163). Cut the nose from bristol board.

3 Color the nose with markers. Punch holes at the dots shown in the pattern below, and insert pipe cleaners through the holes for whiskers.

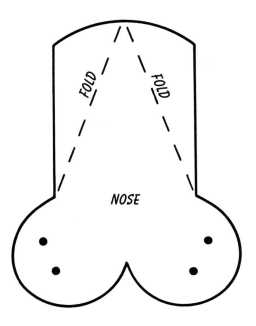

4 Cut triangles for the tip of the nose, ears, and smaller inner ears from felt.

5 Glue the tip of the nose onto the paper nose. Fold the nose along the dotted line shown in the diagram and glue it to the frame as shown.

6 Glue the inner ears, centering them on the ears. Glue the ears to the outer edges of the frames as shown.

K

*droopy jowls and floppy
er, working magic with
t, and paper.*

ıglasses with hard,
frames (glue will not
, opaque plastic)
e-ply bristol board

:ers

1 Trace patterns for nose, jowls, and ears (see "How to Trace and Use Your Patterns," page 163). Cut the nose and jowls from bristol board, the ears from felt.

2 For eyes, trace the outlines of the glass lenses onto typing paper. Cut out four lens shapes.

3 Following the photograph, color one pair of eyes, the nose, and the jowls with markers. To make holes to see through, cut out pupils on each colored eye and its corresponding plain eye.

4 Apply glue to the outer edges of each eye shape and place colored eyes on the outsides and plain eyes on the insides of the lenses, matching up the holes. Glue the jowls to the lower frames, tucking the nose below the bridge, and fasten the ears to the earpieces (temples) as shown.

SHOPPING NOTE: If you cannot find glasses in the shape shown, modify the pattern to fit the lenses you have.

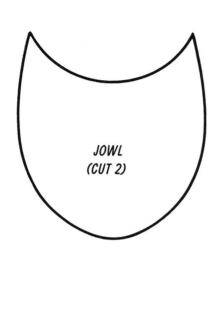

JOWL
(CUT 2)

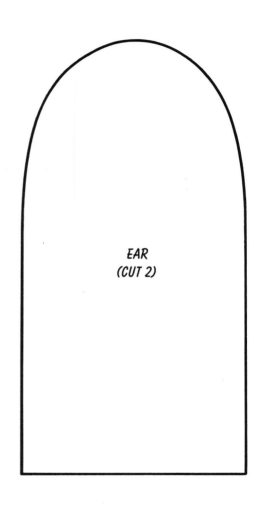

EAR
(CUT 2)

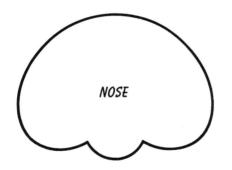

NOSE

EASY GINGERBREAD HOUSES

BEGINNER (HOUSE)

INTERMEDIATE (CHURCH)

Milk cartons, store-bought cookies, and candies are all kids need to have a blast making their own gingerbread houses. It's a great schoolroom project, as well as good family fun.

You will need:

Empty milk cartons, pint-size for
  houses, half-gallon and pint-
  size for church
Graham crackers
Royal Icing (see page 130)
Candies and cereals (such as
  gumdrops, M&M's, hard
  candies, Necco wafers,
  cinnamon candies, small wheat
  squares)
Plastic knife
Masking tape
Stapler
Blunt scissors

For a whole village scene, you will need, in addition:

Pinecones
Colored tissue paper
Coconut flakes
Large square of cardboard
Aluminum foil
Modeling clay
Green poster paint
Paintbrush

1 Wash and dry the cartons. Staple the tops of the pint-size cartons closed.

2 *For the church,* open out the top folds of the half-gallon container. Cut along each corner of the top section as shown in Diagram 1. Cut off the top 1 to 1½ inches of each flap. Fold the top flaps in toward the center to make a neat box end. Tape to hold the flaps in place.

3 Place the half-gallon carton on its side. Place a pint carton at one end for the church steeple, with the front edge flush (even) with the front edge of the larger carton and centered between the side edges of the larger carton (see Diagram 2). Tape the steeple in place.

4 With an adult's help, make Royal Icing (see page 130).

5 With a plastic knife, spread a thin coat of icing over the cartons. Attach graham crackers to the sides and roofs, covering each area as completely as possible. Fill in any spaces with more icing.

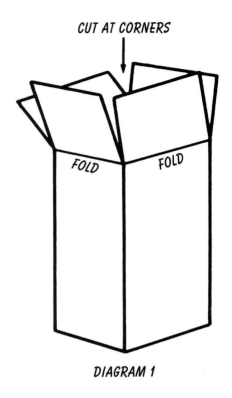

CUT AT CORNERS

FOLD   FOLD

DIAGRAM 1

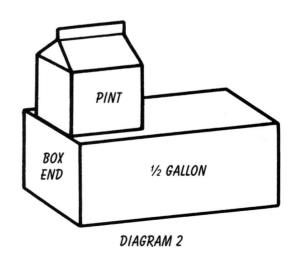

PINT

BOX END   ½ GALLON

DIAGRAM 2

6 For the church's back roof, form an upside down V with two graham crackers, and with icing, cement them together at the peak. Use a generous amount of icing inside the peak to hold the crackers in place. Attach the roof to the back of the church with some more icing.

7 Let the buildings dry overnight (or at least one hour).

8 Decorate the houses and church as you wish, attaching candies and cereals (good for roofs) with more icing.

9 *For a complete village*, cover the cardboard square with aluminum foil. Attach the buildings to the square with small dots of modeling clay.

10 To add some trees, paint the pinecones green. Let the paint dry. Roll bits of colored tissue into small "Christmas balls" and press these between the scales of the painted pinecones to decorate the trees. Put more dots of clay on the square, then place the pinecones stem-side down on them, pushing the stem ends into the clay.

11 Sprinkle coconut flakes over the village to look like snow.

ROYAL ICING

(for Easy Gingerbread Houses)

Warning: Because of a small but very real chance of salmonella contamination from raw egg whites (especially dangerous for children), we strongly recommend using meringue powder or pasteurized dried egg whites instead of raw egg whites. Meringue powder and pasteurized dried egg whites are available from cake-decorating supply stores. Follow the package directions for Royal Icing.

If, however, you are absolutely sure that no one will eat the icing and you wish to use fresh egg whites, use the following recipe:

Whites from three large eggs
½ teaspoon cream of tartar
1 pound confectioners' sugar

In a large bowl beat the egg whites and cream of tartar with an electric mixer until foamy. Gradually add the confectioners' sugar and beat five to seven minutes until glossy, stiff peaks form when the beaters are lifted (turn off mixer before lifting). The recipe makes 2½ cups of icing. When you are not actually working with the icing, keep it covered with a damp cloth to prevent its drying out. To store the icing overnight, place it in an air-tight container and refrigerate.

To thin the icing for spreading, place a small amount in a custard cup. Stir in a few drops of water until the icing is thin enough to spread.

CANDY BAUBLE TREE

BEGINNER

Glue candies to a jar lid and you have a great, quickly-made decoration for the holidays.

You will need:

> Flexible plastic lids from coffee cans
>   or other containers
> Small candies (such as M&M's)
> Tacky glue
> For each ornament, a 6-inch length
>   of gold cord
> Sharp needle with a large eye

1 With an adult's help, use the needle to punch a hole in the rim of the plastic lid. Thread the end of the cord through the hole. Knot the ends together inside the lid, leaving a hanging loop on the outside.

2 With the hanging loop at the top, glue the candies to the lid in the shape of a Christmas tree, using brown candies for the trunk and bright colors for the tree. Let the glue dry.

TOY SOLDIER SPOON DOLL

INTERMEDIATE

This is really just a plastic spoon, dressed up with bits of felt, to hang on a Christmas tree and delight the child who made him.

You will need:

Plastic soup spoon
Scraps of felt in assorted colors
Red and black felt-tipped markers
White glue
6-inch length of string
Blunt scissors

1 With black marker, draw two dots for eyes and a smiling mouth on the bowl of the spoon. Draw red cheek dots with the red marker.

2 Cut a 1½-inch square of felt for the hat. Cut two narrow strips of felt in a different color. Glue the strips crisscrossed onto the hat square. Trim the strip ends to match the corners of the hat. Glue the hat to the top of the spoon. Cut a small oval from felt and glue it to the bottom of the hat for a visor.

3 Cut a 2-inch square of felt for the soldier's tunic. Trim the side edges on a slant so the bottom is smaller than the top. Cut a narrow strip of felt and glue it diagonally across the tunic as shown, trimming the ends to match the tunic edges. Cut three small felt squares and glue to the tunic for buttons.

4 Knot the ends of the string together and glue the knotted ends to the back of the hat for a hanging loop.

NOTE: Follow much the same procedure to make other spoon dolls. In our photo we've coupled the toy soldier with a pretty ice skater.

Popcorn and Gumdrop Wreath

BEGINNER

Slide a piece of popcorn along the wire, then slide on a gumdrop behind it . . . and so it goes, an easy and pleasant pastime for children of all ages.

You will need:

Popcorn
Red and green gumdrops
For each wreath, a 12-inch length of thin wire
For each wreath, a 12-inch length of 7/8-inch-wide ribbon
For each wreath, a 6-inch length of gold cord
Straight pins

1 Pick large, fully popped pieces of popcorn and poke the wire through the center of four of them. Slide the popcorn to the center of the wire.

2 Poke one end of the wire through the center of a red gumdrop and slide the gumdrop to the popcorn. Add a green gumdrop to the other side of the popcorn.

3 Working on each side, continue to slide three or four pieces of popcorn, then a gumdrop onto the wire. Alternate gumdrop colors as you work out to the ends of the wire.

4 Fill the wire almost full, ending with popcorn on one side and a gumdrop on the other. Bring the ends of the wire together to form a circle and twist the ends tightly together. Push one last gumdrop onto the wire ends to hide them.

5 Tie the ribbon into a bow. Stick the bow to the top gumdrop with straight pins.

6 Loop the center of the cord over the wire next to the bow. Knot the ends together for a hanging loop.

Pop-up Santa Card

Discover the trick for making pop-up designs. This isn't difficult, but easier for a child with some craft experience.

You will need:

Construction paper in blue, red,
    white, black, and pink
Star stickers
White glue or glue stick
Black felt-tipped marker
Pencil
Tracing paper
Blunt scissors

1 Cut a 6½-inch by 12-inch piece from blue paper. Fold it in half to make a card.

2 Trace the patterns for the whole Santa, boots, fur trims, mittens, beard, and face (see "How to Trace and Use Your Patterns," page 163). Cut out the shapes.

3 Trace around the patterns and cut Santa and a ½-inch circle (for his nose) from the red paper. Cut the fur trims, a ¾-inch circle (for the hat pompon), and the mittens from the white paper. Cut the face from the pink paper. Cut the boots from the black paper. From the white paper, also cut a 1-inch by 9-inch strip.

4 Following the broken lines on the printed Santa pattern, which show you where to place the pieces, glue the face to the head. Glue on the nose and mark two eye dots with the pen.

5 Glue on the fur trims, hat, pompon, beard, mittens, and boots.

6 Fold Santa in half, from the center top to the center bottom, with the right side out. Fold the tip of each mitten forward.

7 Fold the white strip in half to mark the center. Lay Santa, right side up, over the strip, matching the center folds. Glue Santa in place. Fold under about 1¾ inches at each end of the strip (at the fold in Santa's mittens).

8 Open up the card and lay Santa at the center, along the fold line. Glue the folded-under ends of the strip to the card under Santa's arms. Check that Santa folds forward properly as the card closes.

9 Stick stars to the inside of the card around Santa as shown in the photograph.

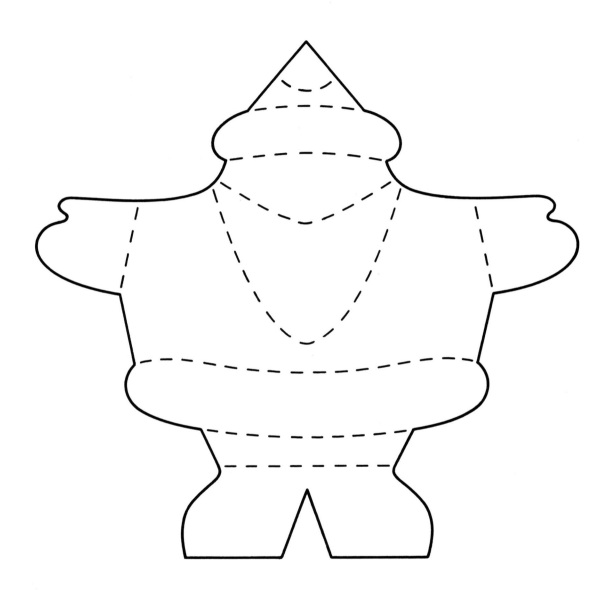

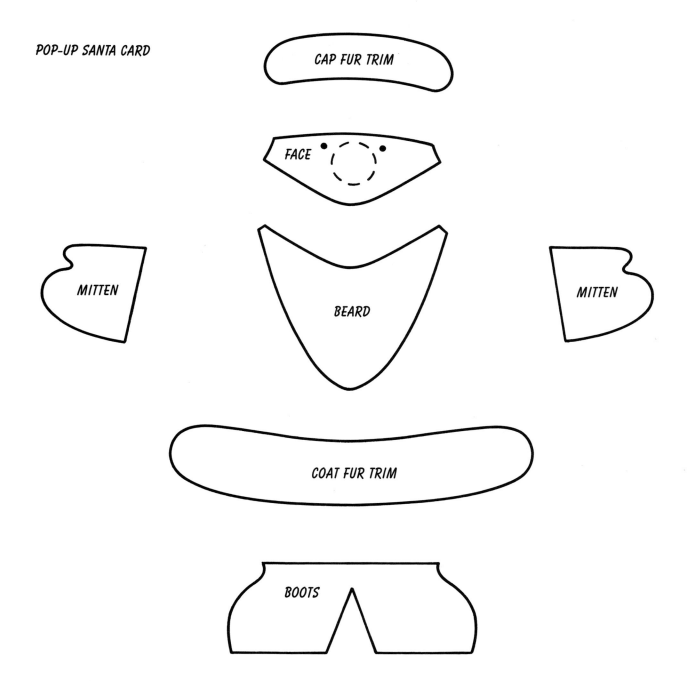

POP-UP SANTA CARD

CAP FUR TRIM

FACE

MITTEN

BEARD

MITTEN

COAT FUR TRIM

BOOTS

Pop-up Christmas Tree Card

INTERMEDIATE

Star stickers and construction paper in five colors give this holiday greeting a bright Christmas look.

You will need:

Construction paper in red, green,
    yellow, pink, and orange
Star stickers
White glue or glue stick
Black felt-tipped marker
Pencil
Tracing paper
Blunt scissors

1 Cut a 6½-inch by 12-inch piece from red paper. Fold it in half to make a card.

2 Trace the patterns for the tree and the star (see "How to Trace and Use Your Patterns," page 163). Cut out the shapes.

3 Trace around the patterns and cut the tree from the green paper and the star from the yellow paper. Cut two ¾-inch-diameter circles each from yellow, pink, and orange paper for balls. Also cut a strip 1½ inches by 9 inches from the red paper.

4 Glue the star to the top of the tree and a ball to each branch point as shown in the picture.

5 Glue the tree over the center of the red strip, matching the bottom edges.

6 Fold the tree and strip in half, from the center top to the center bottom, with the tree side out.

7 Fold under about 1¾ inches at each end of the strip (fold next to the bottom balls).

8 Open up the card and lay the tree at the center along the fold line. Glue the folded-under ends of the strip to the card. Check that the tree folds forward properly as the card closes.

9 Stick a star on the center of each ball, on the star on the tree, and scattered over the center of the tree and the inside of the card around the tree.

Macaroni Star

BEGINNER

Pasta tubes produce this handsome ornament, which even a very young child can make.

You will need:

Pasta tubes, ½ inch in diameter and 2 inches long with diagonally cut ends (we used mostaccioli rigati)
White glue
Cardboard
Gold cord
Blunt scissors

1 From the cardboard, cut a 1½-inch-diameter circle for a base.

2 Cut a 10-inch length of cord. Thread the cord through two pasta tubes. Knot cord ends together for a hanging loop.

3 Spread glue over the cardboard base.

4 Following the diagram, glue the ends of the pasta tubes (including the two with the hanging cord through them) to the base, fitting the points together at the center as shown. Be sure that the hanging loop extends beyond the edge of the design. Let the glue dry completely.

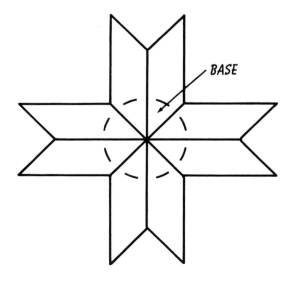

BASE

GLITTER STAR

Glue, Popsicle sticks, and glitter are the ingredients for this contribution to the Christmas tree.

You will need:

Popsicle sticks, five for each star
Glitter
White glue
Gold cord
Brush

1 Spread glue over a flat side of one stick. Following Diagram 1 for how to place the sticks, lay a second stick over the first glued one.

2 Spread glue over the top side of the second stick. Following Diagram 2, add the third stick.

3 Continue to glue the top stick and follow Diagrams 3 and 4 to add the fourth and fifth sticks, forming a five-pointed star.

4 Brush glue over the whole star. While the glue is still wet, sprinkle some glitter over the star. Let the glue dry before lifting the star.

5 Turn the star over, brush this side with glue and sprinkle it with glitter until it is covered. Let the glue dry.

6 Cut a 6-inch piece of cord. Thread the cord through the opening at one point of the star and knot the ends together for a hanging loop.

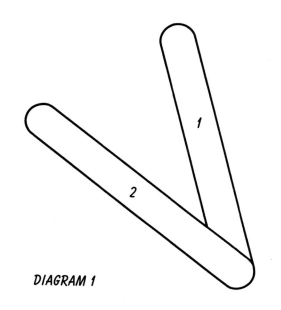

DIAGRAM 1

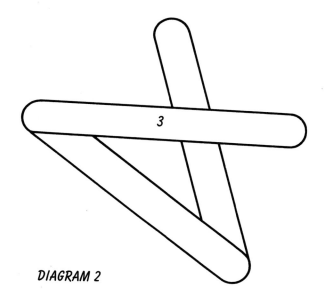

DIAGRAM 2

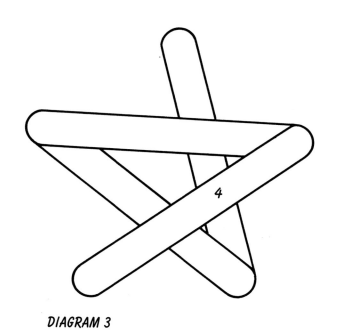

DIAGRAM 3

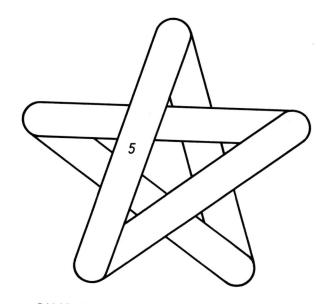

DIAGRAM 4

PAPER SNOWFLAKES

BEGINNER

Snowflakes look heavenly when strung up at a window, the better to be admired by holiday company. The patterns given here make these easy for anyone to cut out.

You will need:

> Pencil
> White typing paper
> Invisible thread (nylon
>   monofilament, available from
>   crafts supply stores)
> Blunt scissors

1 Cut a 6-inch paper square for each snowflake.

2 Fold the paper square in half. Then fold it again in the other direction to make a small square (see Diagram 1, page 148).

3 Fold the square into thirds as follows:
Fold corner Y to the front along the line from A to B. Fold corner X to the back along the dotted line from A to C.

For evenly shaped snowflakes, it is important to fold the square exactly into thirds so that the folds at each side match the turned-back edges. (AC matches AY and AB matches AX exactly at the side edges in Diagram 3.)

4 Cut off the extra paper at the top point, along the broken line X to Y on Diagram 3.

5 Following the broken lines on the diagrams for the snowflakes, lightly pencil cutting lines onto the paper. Keeping the paper folded, cut along the penciled lines, snipping away small areas along the folds. As you cut, be sure to cut through all the layers of paper.

6 Open the piece carefully and flatten it with your fingers.

7 Cut a 10-inch length of the thread. Thread it through an opening near any end point on the snowflake. Knot the thread ends together to form a hanging loop.

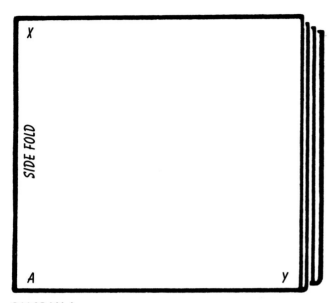

X

SIDE FOLD

A   y

DIAGRAM 1

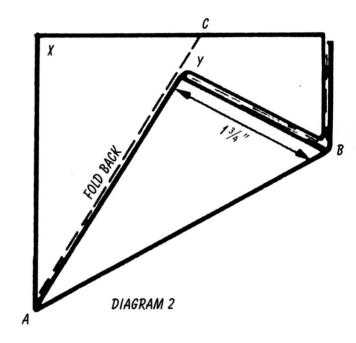

C

X

y

1 3/4 "

FOLD BACK

B

A

DIAGRAM 2

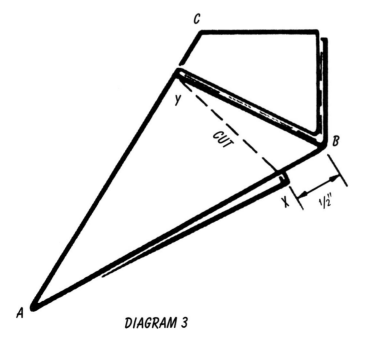

C

y

CUT

B

X

1/2"

A

DIAGRAM 3

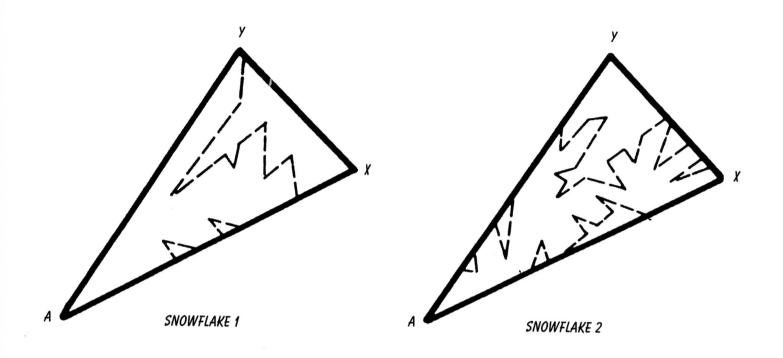

SNOWFLAKE 1

SNOWFLAKE 2

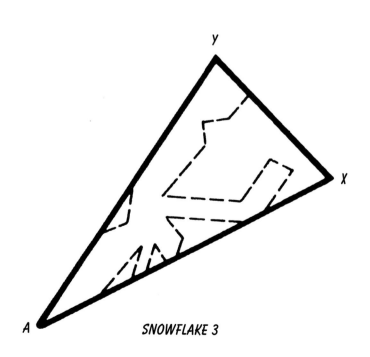

SNOWFLAKE 3

Soda-Straw Ornaments

A whole tree full of these star bursts is handsome, but the ornament also looks grand interspersed with all sorts of traditional decorations.

You will need:

Plastic drinking straws
Thin wire
Blunt scissors

1 For each ornament, cut twelve 6-inch lengths of straws. Cut a 12-inch length of thin wire.

2 Hold the cut straws in a bunch with the ends even. With your other hand, tightly wrap the center of the wire several times around the middle of the bunch of straws. Twist the wires together several times to fasten the straws securely.

3 Bend the straws out from the wired center to form a starburst.

4 Use the wire ends to attach the ornament to your tree.

CANDY BAUBLE SQUARE

Gumdrops on the bottom of an ashtray make quick work of this ornament.

You will need:

Metallic paper ashtray (available in
    party supply stores)
Drinking straw
Gumdrops
White glue
6-inch cord or string
Paper punch

1 Punch a hole at one corner of the rim of the ashtray. Thread the cord through the hole. Tie the cord ends together to form a hanging loop.

2 Cut the straw into 2-inch lengths.

3 Arrange the gumdrops and the cut straws as shown in the photograph, or as you wish, on the bottom of the upside-down ashtray. Glue them in place. Let the glue dry.

General Directions

Adapt the instructions for the Candy Bauble Tree (page 131) to make these colorful ornaments.

HELPING THE YOUNG CRAFTER SUCCEED

GETTING STARTED

Everyone loves to do crafts projects, but when the fun is over, no one wants to clean up. That is why it is so important to start out *covered*. Remember, a little extra time spent in preparation will save a whole lot of time at the end. The kitchen is probably the most practical place to work in, since it not only has a table and chairs, and probably no rug to worry about soiling, but, most important, it has a sink.

Covering the work surface: A plastic tablecloth that is used exclusively for crafts projects will provide the perfect protective table covering. It is cleanable and reusable. However, if you do not have one, there are other ways to ensure maximum protection. A painter's plastic drop cloth (usually 9 feet by 12 feet) can be cut to fit your table. An extra-large (30-gallon) garbage bag, slit down one long side and along the bottom, will open up to cover a large work area. You can use it again if it does not get too messy from a first project. Newspapers work out fine in several layers, but they need to be taped down to avoid too much movement on the table top. If you are also concerned about the floor, even though most paint and glue is easily cleaned away while still wet, lay newspapers or plastic drop cloths down for maximum protection.

Protecting your clothes: It is always advised that children—and adults as well—wear smocks or old shirts with long sleeves cut short to cover their clothes. Most white glues are not washable after they dry (unless otherwise stated on the bottle). Both acrylic and fabric paints dry very hard and do not wash out after they dry.

Protecting your hands: When working with dyes as in the Tie-dyed T-shirts, you must wear plastic gloves to protect your hands. Otherwise the dye will stain your skin.

Setting up supplies: Before you begin to work, read the directions carefully and gather the supplies and containers needed, arranging them so that the items you will be using are near you as you progress with your project.

Remember that even though each project specifies materials needed to make the piece, you can make substitutions and additions of your own. For example, the Paper Bag Clown can be decorated not only with construction paper but with ribbons, yarn, buttons, glitter, feathers, cottonballs, pipe cleaners, and paint—or just about anything you happen to have around the house.

Plastic or small aluminum-foil containers or baby food jars are good for holding small amounts of paint, glue, and other working materials.

If the project calls for paints, keep a can or jar of warm, sudsy water ready to drop paint-brushes in as you finish using them. The brushes will be easier to rinse clean when you are all done.

Always have a saucer with a damp sponge and paper towels on hand to wipe up sticky fingers and excess glue.

Finally, in addition to reading through all project directions first, read directions for each glue to determine the proper method of application, drying time, and cleanup proce-dure *before* you begin!

CLEANUP

When a child's craft project is finished, it is important that it be properly displayed or saved. Items children make themselves can be more important than any purchased posses-sions.

We must also put a high value on the tools and materials we use in our handicrafts. As troublesome as it may be to clean up, doing so is necessary if we are to look forward to a next period of creative fun. In fact, crafts work isn't much fun unless the paper, paints, brushes, and other supplies and tools are well cared for, readily at hand, and ready for use. The child really needs to learn this.

Cleanup is a discipline. Just as the child be-comes educated in the step-by-step process of a crafts project, he or she must learn a step-by-step routine that makes it easy to put things away.

First, you should have a wastebasket or pail (or both, as needed) for wet waste in the child's work space, so the child can dispose of some scraps as he or she goes along.

But cleanup entails a lot more than throw-ing out waste. In fact, this is a good place to teach a little conservation.

Your youngster should have good tools and good materials to work with. Even if they are inexpensive, he or she should be aware that they are valuable. Teach your child to save ma-terials for reuse or to use in new items he or she may dream up. This requires a storage system.

Make sure your young crafter knows *where* things belong. Even if you have limited stor-age space, you might have one box labeled CRAFTS SUPPLIES for all the materials—yarn, feathers, buttons, bows, shells, and the like. Another box, labeled ART SUPPLIES, can be used to store paints, brushes, crayons, pencils, paper, cardboard, and so forth.

A fairly young child can also help with stor-age ideas. For example, he or she can paint and label shoeboxes for the collected supplies and tools, which are then easy to move from the child's room to the kitchen or the porch if either of those is a favorite place to work.

Muffin tins and ice cube trays are also help-ful, not only to organize small items like but-tons and beads, but to use right at the work table, without having to unpack anything first.

Good labeling is part of smart storage, but take advantage of clear containers, too. These make quick work of spotting what you are looking for.

Some tools used in crafts projects are also used by the family in maintenance or repair projects around the house, so you need rules for putting these back where they belong after use.

But it's a very good idea for the child to have his or her own basic tools—for example, a scissors and ruler.

Children should have paintbrushes of their own, too, that they themselves learn to keep in shape and store correctly with their art materials. They should be taught to clean paintbrushes after each use. Otherwise, neglect will cause the paint to harden in the hairs, or the brush will spread out of shape. Brushes should be washed in soapy water and then rinsed in clear water. Shape the hairs with your fingers and rest them on a paper towel to dry, or stand them brush-side up in a container.

Help your child realize that cleanup is something you do in preparation for having fun the next time around.

The Easy Gingerbread Houses on pages 126 through 130 can be a good class or group project for children of all ages.

EVERYTHING YOU NEED TO KNOW WHEN BUYING SUPPLIES OR TOOLS

PAPER AND BOARDS

Typing paper: Common nonerasable white 8½-inch by 11-inch sheets of typing paper are available at variety stores, stationery stores, and even grocery stores. It comes in tablets or packages. Although the paper is too thin for paint, it can be used for work with markers, crayons, Cray-pas, and colored pencils.

Construction paper: This all-purpose, inexpensive paper is available almost anywhere, even in grocery stores. You can find it in pads or packages. It comes in white and assorted colors. The size varies from 9-inch by 12-inch sheets to 12-inch by 18-inch sheets, and larger sheets can be found in art supply stores.

You can never have enough construction paper, so don't worry about having any left over after a project is completed.

Construction paper is easy to tear or cut with scissors, easy to glue, and is suitable for collages. You can draw on it with markers, crayons, or Cray-pas. Colored pencils and painting markers work best on white paper.

Fadeless™: This is a bristol-type paper also available in a poster board or construction paper weight. It is found in variety and large chain department stores. The Fadeless that is similar to construction paper comes in assorted colors and sizes and can be used for paper sculpture, drawing, painting, and collages. It is relatively inexpensive and won't crack when creased or folded.

Brown wrapping paper: Brown wrapping paper is found in most variety stores and places where gift wraps are sold. It is used primarily to wrap packages for mailing, but, because of its reasonable cost, it is ideally suited for our Sponge-Print Wrapping Paper (see page 90). Crayons, Cray-pas, and all paints will take to its surface and, because of its size, it is suited for making murals.

Don't forget you can also use brown sandwich bags and large grocery bags to print, paint, and draw on.

Tracing paper: This transparent paper is sold in pads of various sizes in stationery stores and art supply stores. It is recommended for tracing patterns given in this book (see "How to Trace and Use Your Patterns," page 163).

Poster board: This multi-purpose paper is also widely available. It is often called oak tag or railroad board. The sheets are large, about 22 inches by 28 inches, and come in white and a variety of colors.

The surface is smooth and ideal for taking felt-tipped markers and both acrylic and poster paints. Both paints sit well on this cardboard-like paper, which is a little heavier than bristol board and a little lighter than shirt cardboard. Crayons don't work so well on it, because the surface is too slick for the waxiness of the crayon. Poster board can be cut with a good pair of sharp scissors or a craft knife. Parental supervision is recommended when cutting, however.

Bristol board: This heavyweight paper comes in a variety of thicknesses, but you need be concerned only about two-ply bristol board. It is heavier than construction paper and lighter than poster board. It comes in pads or sheets and can be found in most art supply and hobby shops. You can use any paint on it, as well as crayons, pens, pencils, and either white or tacky glue. It is thin enough to cut easily with a good pair of scissors.

GLUES

Glue stick: The glue stick is a no-mess material that is ideal for the preschooler. Although it won't work on everything, it allows younger children greater freedom to work away, compared with the mess they can make with white glue. Use the stick for paper projects, like the Valentine cards, Christmas pop-up cards, and desk set described in this book.

A glue stick is the simplest glue to use, but it does not have the durability of other glues. It can really be used successfully only with paper.

White glue: This widely available glue is the one most often used for crafts projects of all kinds. It bonds most porous and semiporous materials. It is perfect for all paper products, fabrics like cotton and felt, and even yarns and ribbon. It is also an excellent bonding agent for plastic foam, wood, and pebbles. It dries clear and relatively fast. (See "How to Work with Glue," page 165.)

Tacky glue: Tacky glue is basically a thicker version of white glue and is used when a project requires quick adhering and no movement. Because it dries fast, it is recommended when you require extreme tackiness and good holding power. It bonds wood, metal, cloth, plastic foam, even fabric. For example, the Wind Sock on page 60 calls for tacky glue to hem the edges. Although white glue would usually be used to glue fabric, tacky glue is recommended here to ensure the strength and durability of the Wind Sock.

Tacky glue is readily available and must be worked with quickly and cleaned up before it dries. Because it is difficult to squeeze out of a bottle or tube, younger children will need help with its application.

Household cement: There are many household cements available, and they are all used for home crafts repairs. They bond china, glass, shells, metal, ceramics, tile, leather, wood, most plastics, and many other materials.

This glue must be used with adult supervision because it is flammable and gives off toxic fumes. However, because it is so quick-drying, creates so strong a bond on the materials mentioned above, and dries crystal clear, we use it for certain projects.

Nail polish remover will clean it up, but

cover your clothes and work area to minimize the necessity for cleanup.

Epoxy: When a very strong and waterproof bond is required, a five-minute epoxy is excellent—because it dries in five minutes.

Epoxy comes in two tubes, one a resin and the other a hardener, which you mix together in equal quantities. Since it dries quickly, remember to mix only the amount needed at one time.

We have not recommended epoxy in the instructions throughout this book, because it should be used only by adults and older, responsible children. But it would be useful for a project like the Shell Pins and Magnets (page 44).

PAINT

Acrylic paints: Acrylics are being used more and more for crafts projects. They are available in art supply stores in a variety of colors, in either tube or jar.

These plastic paints can be thinned with water. They are durable and cover almost any surface, including wood, hardened clay, stones, eggs, beach shells, twigs, and nuts. Acrylic paint is also good on poster board and bristol board and is ideal for either sponging or painting with a brush. It dries to a very hard finish and can be coated with a gloss or matte acrylic varnish for items that need a durable finish or might get wet, like the clay Soap Dish on page 86.

Check labels for toxicity. Some acrylics are toxic. Ask for nontoxic acrylics when buying paint for use by young children. (See "How to Use Acrylic Paints," page 165.)

Poster (tempera) paint: For many years, this was the only paint used for children's crafts projects. It is still used in nursery schools and elementary schools because it is water-soluble, nontoxic, and washable.

It is perfect paint for construction paper, cardboard, and poster or bristol boards. It is, however, less permanent than acrylic and does not cover nearly as many surfaces as does acrylic. Also, even after it dries, if splashed with water, it will run, unless it is coated with a varnish.

Poster paint can be purchased in powder form or already premixed and is available in variety stores and hobby and art supply stores.

Fabric paint: This is used exclusively for printing, painting, or sponging on fabric. It is an acrylic paint that remains colorfast even after many washes. There are many available brands, sold in art supply stores and some variety stores.

Some fabric paints come in a tube with a nozzle for easy application of the paint. By squeezing the tube and guiding the tip you can transform your clothes into custom-decorated creations. You can use it on T-shirts, sneakers, hats, and other fabric items that need a colorful touch.

These paints have the bright look of enamel. Some contain glitter, and a puff paint variety produces a three-dimensional look when heated. We show puff paint on T-shirts and sneakers (pages 68 and 69.)

TOOLS

A tool can be anything from a toothpick to a kitchen spoon.

For many of the projects in this book, a pair of blunt safety scissors is the only tool needed. Some projects, however, require sharper scissors, a craft knife, or special tools. For these projects we recommend adult supervision and assistance. Parents working one-on-one with a child may find it possible to teach even a young child how to use these tools correctly and carefully, so that the child can learn to work on the projects more independently. Let your knowledge of your child's motor skills and ability to follow safety rules be your guide.

Scissors: Scissors are used for many projects and are considered to be a standard supply item. It is important that scissors be used properly by young children and that the correct scissors be given to a young child.

Blunt scissors, sometimes referred to as safety scissors, have both blades rounded and are good for the very young. They are generally used to cut construction paper, magazines, newsprint, and the like.

Pointed scissors have both blades pointed and are good for precise cutting. They may be used by older children or responsible younger children who will handle them correctly.

Note that you can buy scissors specially made for those who are left-handed. (Most scissors are made for people who are right-handed.) If your child is left-handed, ask for "left-handed" blunt scissors.

Vinyl-coated handles make some scissors easier on the fingers.

Craft knives: The craft knife is used when an absolutely clean cut is required or when a cut is being made in an area where scissors cannot reach. The Jumping Jack toy (see page 30) requires a craft knife if an exact cut is to be achieved. However, this does not mean that the toy cannot be made if you don't own a craft knife, merely that the finish of the cut will not be the same. The Eraser-Print Stationery, on the other hand, must be done with a craft knife (see page 92), and we suggest that the supervising adult be the one to make these cuts.

There are three basic styles of craft knives, each durable and safe when handled properly. These multi-purpose precision knives can all be used for cutting cardboard and for carving or shaving pieces of wood, plastic foam, cork, and other materials.

The utility knife can be found in hardware stores, variety stores, paint stores, and home improvement centers. It has a sturdy aluminum handle and comes equipped with blades that are easily inserted.

The second type of craft knife has an aluminum handle similar to a pen. Like the utility knife, it holds securely any of a variety of blades that are bought separately.

Snap-off blade knives are the most economical knives available. In the handle is a long incised blade that can be snapped off when the cutting edge is dull. These blades can be bought separately and are easily inserted into the handle. The blade retracts for safety when not in use.

Saws: The only saws needed for the few projects with dowels would be a hacksaw or very small hand saw. The plywood or pine base for the String Picture (see page 84) can be cut with a hacksaw, but it would be faster for Mom or Dad to use a jigsaw. If you go to the lumberyard for scrap wood, ask the workers there to cut the wood to size for you.

Drills: There are only two projects in this book that call for any drilling—the Stretchable Crocodile and Clown (page 38) and the Shell and Pompon Snake (page 50). A simple hand drill or power drill with a small-diameter bit can be used for the holes to be made there. We recommend that an adult supervise any older child using a drill and do the actual drilling for a younger child.

BRUSHES

Brushes for children are sold in places you'd hardly expect—the grocery store, the drugstore—and, of course, in art supply, variety, and stationery stores. Usually you can find a package of six or eight brushes at a reasonable cost.

Brushes come in a variety of sizes, and it is advisable to have three sizes on hand—fine, medium, and wide. The brushes that come packaged together are generally made from soft hairs and are suitable for poster paints and acrylics that are thinned with water. A stiffer brush made of a material like nylon is recommended for acrylics that have not been thinned.

Sable brushes are excellent for acrylic and poster paints, but they are expensive and not necessary for the crafts projects given in this book.

Shell pins made using the instructions on page 44 are distinctive additions to any young lady's outfit.

BASIC CRAFTS SKILLS

HOW TO TRACE AND USE YOUR PATTERNS

Lay a sheet of transparent tracing paper over the printed pattern in the book. With a pencil, trace over all the pattern lines and marked dots. If the instructions say to make separate patterns for each unit, as for the Full-of-Beans Bear (page 20), trace the whole outline first. Then on another sheet of tracing paper, trace each of the details. Cut out all the traced shapes to make the patterns.

Lay the pattern on the paper or fabric you want to cut the shape from. If you are using fabric, pin the pattern to the fabric with straight pins. Holding the pattern firmly in place, with a soft pencil trace around the edge of the pattern to mark the outline on the paper or fabric. Cut out the shapes.

HOW TO BRAID

Divide strands of yarn into three equal groups. Bring the right strand over the center strand and drop in the middle (Diagram 1). Bring the left strand over the center strand and drop it in the middle (Diagram 2). Bring the right strand to the center (Diagram 3). Continue alternating, bringing the left strand, then the right strand to the center to make the braid (Diagram 4).

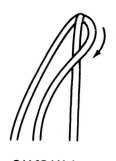 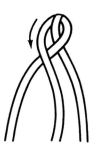  

DIAGRAM 1   DIAGRAM 2   DIAGRAM 3   DIAGRAM 4

Note the difference in design and texture in this Found-Object Picture Rubbing compared to the photograph on page 95.

HOW TO WORK WITH GLUE

Applying glue: Most glue bottles have applicator caps and should be wiped clean after each use. To further prevent clogging, make sure the cap is screwed closed when you're finished using it.

Some children will be able to work with the bottle directly and control the flow of glue successfully. But for those little hands that cannot manage the bottle, just pour a small amount of glue into a jar lid and use a toothpick—or a cotton swab or a narrow paintbrush—as an applicator. The best advice, when working with glue, is to use as little as is necessary.

Wash your hands frequently if they get sticky so that your project stays clean. Apply glue to both items being glued, as when fixing the nose on the Spool Doll or the eyes and nose on the Shell Pins and Magnets.

Drying time: Whatever glue you use, remember that drying time depends on the amount used and also on the room temperature. High humidity slows down drying time.

It is important to exercise patience when using glue. Many a craft project has been ruined by not allowing the glue sufficient time to dry.

Children can learn to wait for glue to dry. Teach them to use "a little bit" of glue for small or delicate gluing. Counting to ten while holding an object in place allows the glue to set. Some projects should not be moved while the glue is drying.

Make sure that the glue you buy is nontoxic and gives off no harmful fumes (see page 159 for a review of types of glues used in crafts projects). Some white glues are completely washable. This means that they can be washed out of clothing even after they have dried. If you cannot find completely washable glue, make sure that your clothes are sufficiently covered while working. Clean up your work area with warm water and a sponge before any spilled glue hardens.

HOW TO USE ACRYLIC PAINTS

When using acrylic paint, it is most important to keep it from drying out. Pour or squeeze the paint into a small container with a lid to keep the paint from drying out and to provide handy storage for the leftover paint. Film and pill containers, as well as baby food jars, are useful for holding both acrylic and poster paints.

If possible, have a separate paintbrush available for each different color of paint you are using. Otherwise, wash the brush and wipe off excess water with a white paper towel before using it for a different color.

Before applying the paint add a few drops of water, as needed, to get it to the consistency of heavy cream. Now you are ready to begin.

When you are through painting, be sure to clean up the brushes with warm soapy water *before* the paint dries.

If you get acrylic paint on your clothes, wash it out quickly with soap and water before it dries. Otherwise it will not come off.

These distinctive paperweights or desk ornaments can all be made by using the instructions given on page 82.

INDEX

SELECTING PROJECTS TO SUIT THE YOUNG CRAFTER'S SKILLS

BEGINNER
CANDY BAUBLE TREE
CANDY BAUBLE SQUARE
CANDY-COATED EGGS
CRAYON-STRIPED EGGS
DESK SET
DINOSAUR PINS
EASY GINGERBREAD HOUSES
FOLDED-HANDS VALENTINE
FOUND-OBJECT PICTURE RUBBING
FRUIT AND VEGETABLE PRINTS
GLITTER STAR
HANGING BASKET
HEART STICKERS POT
LEAF PRINTS
LEAF RUBBING
LOVING CUP
MACARONI STAR
NEWSPAPER HAT
PAPER BAG CLOWN
PAPER SNOWFLAKES
POPCORN AND GUMDROP WREATH
PRETEND BEACH SAILBOAT
PUFF-PAINT SNEAKERS

PUFF-PAINT SWEATSHIRT
SHADOW DRAWING
SPECKLED EGGS
SPONGE-PRINT EGGS
SPONGE-PRINT WRAPPING PAPER
STICKER EGGS
STICKER LOTTO
STRING PICTURE
TICK-TACK-TOE GAME
VALENTINE CROWN
WATER SCOPE

INTERMEDIATE
BEAN NECKLACE
BUTTON NECKLACE AND BARRETTE
DUDLEY SPOOL DRAGON
EASY GINGERBREAD CHURCH
ERASER-PRINT STATIONERY
FULL-OF-BEANS BEAR
HOUND MASK
KITTEN MASK
PAPERWEIGHTS
PEA AND TOOTHPICK CREATION
POP-UP CHRISTMAS TREE CARD

POP-UP SANTA CARD
SAND SUNBURST
SHELL CATCHALL
SHELL AND FEATHER ANIMALS
SHELL AND POMPON SNAKE
SHELL PINS AND MAGNETS
SODA-STRAW ORNAMENTS
TINY SPOOL DOLLS
TOY SOLDIER SPOON DOLL

EXPERIENCED
BIRDS IN BRANCHES
BREAD-DOUGH FLOWER EGGS
CRACKED-SHELL EGGS
JUMPING JACK
ROCK VILLAGE
SAND CASTLE PENCIL HOLDER
SOAP DISH
STRETCHABLE CROCODILE AND CLOWN
TERRARIUM
TIE-DYED T-SHIRTS
WIND SOCK
WOODEN-SPOON PUPPETS

All of us at Meredith® Press are dedicated to offering you, our customer, the best books we can create. We are particularly concerned that all of the instructions for making the projects are clear and accurate. We welcome your comments and would like to hear any suggestions you may have. Please address your correspondence to Customer Service Department, Meredith® Press. Meredith Corporation, 150 East 52nd Street, New York, NY 10022.